The Silk Cotton Tree

Douen

Largahoo

Papa Bois

Soucouyant

La Diablesse

Mama Glo

Jumbie Come to Meet You

A guide to pronunciation

Douen – Dwen

Largahoo – La-ga-who

Papa Bois – Papa bwa

Soucouyant – Soo-coo-ya

La Diablesse – La-ja-bless

Mama Glo –

Jumbie in Town

David Kalloo

Jumbie in Town

Published by David Kalloo

©Copyright David Kalloo 2021

This book is based on factual events in my childhood and teenage years.

Names and dates have been omitted for the purpose of

identification of anyone living or deceased.

British Library Cataloguing-in-Publication Data

A catalogue record for this book is available on request from the British library.

ISBN ISBN: 979-8529425077

© David Kalloo

Published 2021

Cover Design by: cashewmedia

Jumbie in Town

Jumbie in Town is a biographical account of my childhood and teenage years when I embarked on a journey to find Jumbies depicted in the Trinidad and Tobago folklore.

I have chosen refrain from using names to protect the identity of anyone mentioned in the book, who may be alive or deceased. Careful consideration has been taken in the description of anyone mentioned in the book. Any reference or likeness to anyone living or deceased are purely coincidental.

Where dates and names are used, this has been done purely for historical context only, in the narration of the story. The account, in this book reflects only my lived experiences during my quest to find a Jumbie in town.

Jumbie in Town

Trinidad and Tobago are a duet-island country that is a rich amalgamated cultural melting pot, brimming with colourful characters of folklores that could make you laugh, cry and tremble with fear. Common were tales of Papa Bois, Soucouyant, La Diablesse, Douens, Largahoo, Mama Glo and even Silk Cotton trees, noted for where evil spirits congregate. These tales had the tendency to make you cringe and send shivers down your spine, frightening the living daylights out of you when darkness crept in. These folklores are all an integral part of the cultural myriad of Trinidad and Tobago. If you grew up without knowing, or even hearing at least one of these stories, it means you have missed a great slice of our cultural identity. The folklore stories of these supernatural creatures are so embedded in the culture of Trinidad and Tobago that they have been depicted in carnival costume traditions from the early days of carnival, enduring to present day. Incorporating these folklore legends in the carnival arts has helped to keep folklore alive and cognitive in the minds of both the ageing population and new generation of Trinbagonians.

As a young boy I loved listening to these stories being narrated by elders such as parents, grandparents, uncles, aunts, or even older siblings. Listening to the tales of a Largahoo, Douen or any other supernatural creatures would send shivers down your spine, and had you trembling with fear. Especially as a child, but more so if you lived out the countryside where electricity was non-existent, where darkness brought the most eerie noises from the nearby bushes and forests.

My mother was an excellent narrator of these 'Jumbie' stories – the colloquial term by which these tales are known. At times I was scared but became more intrigued than frightened by these folklores. We lived at the edge of a forest in Arima, east Trinidad, that was also home to a small settlement of the island's indigenous Carib people. Back in those days, we had no electricity. The only electric light was from a streetlamp about 1000 kilometres away from the street where we lived. Even pipe-borne water was a luxury for many of the residents in our little village. We fetched water from a standpipe with metal buckets, about the same distance away as the streetlamp.

Once my mother had finished relating a story at night, she would blow out the kerosene lamp, secure you under the mosquito net, leaving you to drift off to sleep. I would lay in bed with my eyes closed, allowing my imagination to run wild with snapshots of the tale that night. In the forest next to our house, the cacophony of noises from the jungle seemed to seep into the house like an invading mist, from one of those black and white horror movies. I dared not open my eyes, fearing what may present itself before me. You could just form in your mind a picture of this mist, standing upright in front of you like Frankenstein, laughing and waiting to consume you into hell once you opened your eyes. So, you just kept your eyes shut, until the safety of morning arrived.

These folklore stories, in my opinion, were concocted to keep children on the straight and narrow. And in the case of demons such as La Diablesse, Largahoo and Soucouyant, I have a strong inclination that they were fabricated to deter men from overindulging in alcohol, so they could return to their families and homes without being totally inebriated and penniless. Largahoo and La Diablesse could have been the work of clever elders, who could use these tales as excuses for infidelity. Papa Bois and Mama Glo, as you will learn, only protected the forest and its wildlife inhabitants. It was uncommon to hear that Papa Bois had caused death or serious injury to anyone. Mama Glo, it is said, had caused the drowning of some men who followed her into deep basins at riversides.

There were Soucouyant stories too, where women would lift their hems to show the neighbour over the fence the bruised marks on their thighs, cleavage, and other intimate areas, claiming 'Soucouyant suck them' while they slept. The strangest thing that I noticed as a young boy; I had never heard men complained that Soucouyant had sucked them. The only man I can recall claiming to be sucked by a Soucouyant was a calypsonian who sang a catchy tune with the lyrics, '*Suck meh Soucouyant, suck meh…*' This calypso, I must add, contained sexual innuendos.

I must have been about ten years old when the urge to put these myths to the test became deeply imbedded in my mind. My fear of the dead, ghosts, and folklore stories diminished when my stepfather died at home. He died in what seemed like the middle of the night, but it could have well been 11pm or even three in the morning. The place was pitch black and the cry of the forest was very alive with a constant mysterious din. The forest was always very much alive once darkness arrived. By then, you were nestled in the safety of the house with your supper, and if you were lucky, a cup of home-made hot chocolate made from ground cocoa beans and formed into little batons and allowed to dry in the sun before putting into storage. I would watch my mum grate the chocolate, cinnamon stick and nutmeg then add water and put on the fireside to boil. The aroma that emanated from this brew was just heavenly. Try as I may when I got old enough to do it myself, I never got the same heavenly scent.

My mother woke me the night of my stepfather's passing, put a lit flambeau in my hand, then instructed me with careful instructions to go fetch the neighbour who lived about 500 metres away from our house. It was the most surreal experience of my life at the time. I stood speechless in the middle of the gravel road, a dome of light from the flambeau encapsulating me. The edge of the forest on one side, a dead body in the house on the other and pitch-black night ahead of me towards the neighbour's house.

I began to cry and could not move – or wouldn't, I couldn't tell which – petrified not by the dead body in the house or the encroaching noises from the forest, but of the darkness ahead of me. The road ended a short distance in front of me, then the path that led to the neighbour's house was along a small track, with the forest overhanging on both sides. My mother, after several minutes of making me suffer, came out to console me. She brought me inside the house holding me to her chest. I knew she was crying. I could feel her tears trickling down on my head. She grabbed my little face in both hands saying to me, be brave, sit on the bed with your sister. She took the flambeau, lifted it into the air, heading off to get the neighbour.

Sitting on the fibre mattress next to my sleeping sister, my chin buried into my hands, I stared at the dead body on the next bed. The strange noises from the forest were creeping into the house. Fear had gripped me now: I was sure at any moment that the dead body would rise with outstretched hands and attack me. Voices outside the house began to cancel out the forest noise as I heard my mother returning with two of the neighbours.

I was confused at the time as to why my mother never called the neighbour living next door to us. When the figures entered the house, both neighbours were there. The neighbour's husband examined the body and I heard him say, "Gyul the old man gone yes". My mother began to cry quietly, then she let out a pitiful scream that will live with me forever. At that age, I was incapable of comprehending why she screamed, but as I grew older, I gathered that the reality of the death of her husband, dealt a devasting blow. She had never worked a day in her life; with two young children already, and knowing she was with child again must have been a very frightening experience to deal with as a young woman.

My stepfather's body was taken away later in the day and returned at some point later to the house in an aluminium box, packed with ice. I cannot remember how long the body remained in the house, but I do remember a bucket being placed on the floor to collect the water from the melting ice.

I do not recall what sparked my interest in challenging the authenticity of these folklore stories. However, at first when I started my search it was just camping out in the forest. I constructed makeshift tents from palm leaves to stay up all night to witness any encounter with demons such as Largahoo or La Diablesse. I paid a heavy price for my actions from a thick leather belt that once belonged to my stepfather. My mother was merciless with the belt. My gentle, tender skin was always bruised and sore after each episode with the belt. These beatings didn't deter me in the slightest. In fact, it did more to spur me on rather than acting as a deterrent. For as soon as the opportunity presented itself, I was off Jumbie hunting again.

Initially, when I began looking for these Jumbies, I just went into the forest aimlessly, hoping by chance that I would encounter Papa Bois or a Douen or even a Largahoo or maybe a Soucouyant flying about. It had taken several appointments with the leather belt for me to finally work out a method by which I could track down these Jumbies. And so, I began to focus on investigating one Jumbie at a time. With that in mind, I thought what better way to start than by visiting the place where dead people 'lived' and where they spent most of their time: the cemetery. I soon realised that it was not the place to look for anything supernatural. Cemeteries were a desolate and lonely place that had one characteristic, silence. Yet films and stories of the living dead made us scared of the burial grounds. I was no different from the average person who had fears of the cemetery.

One night, it would have been after the Catholic event of All Saints when the graves in the cemetery were cleaned, and people went to light candles for the dead. I ventured up to the Catholic cemetery in Arima and sat on a tombstone and waited to see if any Jumbie would appear. I had no idea what the time was, but I was sure it was well past midnight. The scent of burnt candles still permeated the air. I sat on a tombstone, fashioning a pose like the boy in 'Pip and the Convict' story from my school reading. I sat there and waited. Maybe two hours had passed, maybe less, I couldn't tell, but nothing appeared.

I sat there, waiting and contemplating. I thought maybe these Jumbies were tired after so much commotion in the cemetery the night before. Since the death of my stepfather, I no longer feared the dead. I took consolation, too, from my mother's words, "It's not the dead you have to be afraid off, it's dem *nemakarams* (ungrateful) that living". She would often say this, and I believe there was much sarcasm in her words. "When de dead bury and gone, yuh only left with the living to ketch yuh ass". My mother used to come out with some profound statements that I only understood late in my adulthood.

As I reflected on her words, I could hear voices on the other side of the cemetery. I jumped off the tombstone moving closer, with caution, like a cat on a hunt, stalking its prey. I moved silently to the direction where the voices were coming from. I felt my pocket to ensure that I had my garlic cloves. A stab of fright ran through me realising that they must have fallen out of my pocket as I sat on the tombstone. Moving closer, I got a strong whiff of marijuana in the air. I thought to myself, dead people smoking weed? Ahead of me sitting on a tomb, I could see two figures casually chatting and puffing away on their marijuana joints.

It was not my intention to approach them, so I snuck off quietly without being noticed. As I meandered through the streets of Arima making my way home, I remembered stories about Silk Cotton trees. Folklore has it that under these majestic, innocent looking trees, evil spirits congregated. It is said too, that should you chop a Silk Cotton tree at the stroke of midnight, it bleeds blood. And so, my adventures in search of these folklore Jumbies began.

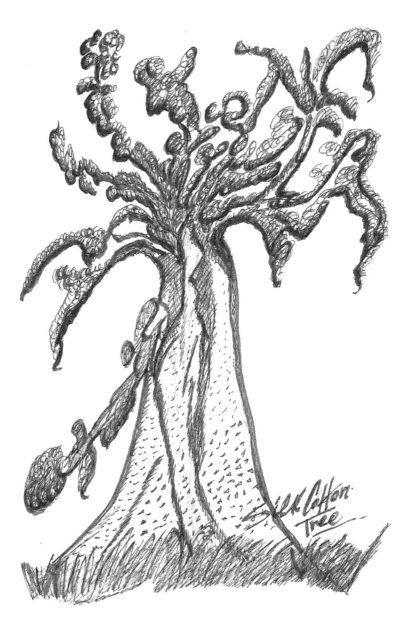

The Silk Cotton Tree

The Silk Cotton Tree

My first real investigation started when I set out, full of enthusiasm to prove, to myself whether Silk Cotton trees produced blood when chopped at midnight. I had heard many stories, from my mother as well as others, that whoever dared to cut down a Silk Cotton tree suffered severe illnesses and even death. Those who were struck down, never seemed to recover from their illness and eventually died.

One of the most notable of these stories was of the man who was hired to fell a Silk Cotton tree in the heart of Sangre Grande. Before the Silk Cotton tree could be cut down, a Hindu priest had come to offer prayers and bless the woodcutter to protect him from any demonic curses that may possess him. There were frantic pleas from some of the people gathered to leave the tree alone. These humble pleas were ignored, and the huge Silk Cotton tree was timbered.

Not long after the tree had been cut down, it was alleged that the woodcutter fell seriously ill, and subsequently died from his short illness. Whether this was as a direct result of him cutting down the Silk Cotton tree, I cannot say, but many people in Sangre Grande said the curse of the Silk Cotton tree killed him for sure. On the spot where the tree once stood, a cinema was built and aptly named, Silk Cinema. It was claimed that the cinema was haunted by evil spirits. There were many reports of spirits wondering about in the ungodly hours of the night in the area. Some even claimed to have seen spirits inside the cinema.

Many years later, before the cinema eventually closed. I went to see a movie there. You could see bats flying about in front of the screen as you watched the movie. Apart from the bats flying about and the cockroaches that scurried about your feet, I didn't experience any supernatural feeling or presence of anything to warrant it being haunted. Putting the threat of being struck down with a severe illness or the fear of death behind me, I embarked on chopping a Silk Cotton tree at midnight. I was prepared: nothing could deter me from carrying out this task. To disprove these myths in folklore, I had to plan carefully. The nearest Silk Cotton tree to where we lived was in dense forest. I could not tell the time then but knew what position of the hands on the clock represented midnight. I needed a torch, a clock, and a cutlass for this expedition and more importantly, a route in the dark to this unholy tree.

We collected firewood in those days from the nearby forest to use in our clay fireside, a *chulha* as my mother called it, where all our meals were prepared. My mother seldom used the green two-burner kerosene stove for cooking. So, collecting firewood was a regular weekend chore. The neighbour's boys and I would scour the woods, returning later with huge bundles of firewood on our heads. We would spend almost half the day gathering firewood and hunting brown doves.

Each time I went to the forest to collect firewood, I cleared a pathway to the Silk Cotton tree until I felt comfortable getting to it in the dead of night. Having all this plan afoot, there was still the task of sneaking out from the house to fulfil this expedition. This proved even more difficult than anticipated. Chiefly because my mother was always up late or, I would fall asleep. The mornings following my unplanned slumber would be heavy with annoyance at myself.

The idea of getting to that Silk Cotton tree had to be abandoned after several attempts failed to materialise. Sadly, sleep came to me, waiting for my mother to retire to bed. For now, the Silk Cotton tree was safe from the well-honed blade I had prepared for the task. It only meant that for the moment, the idea had to be shelved. I had to implement a different plan to carry out the Silk Cotton tree experiment.

My mother had grown weary of my haunts which often resulted in me missing a lot of schooling. So, to keep me on the straight and narrow, ensuring I got an education, she moved me to live with an uncle in San Juan. Here, I was presented with the perfect opportunity to chop a Silk Cotton tree. Not far from where I was staying was a huge Silk Cotton tree. This tree was not as big as the one I first selected, yet it would have taken about three people linking arms to form a circle around its trunk. This was a majestic Silk Cotton tree, standing silently like a sentinel, near a river with huge bamboo clusters on both sides of the riverbank.

I listened as my cousins related stories of how there was evil spirits under the tree. It was my assumption that they were trying to scare me when they said voices could be heard there, even in the daytime. My cousins could only have heard this through stories. None of them were brave enough to venture near this Silk Cotton tree, day, or night, to report on such activities.

One of the advantages with this Silk Cotton tree was that it wasn't difficult to access. The tree was just a few hundred yards from where my uncle lived. There was a clear track, leading directly to the Silk Cotton tree. Even in the dark, you could gain access to the tree without having to negotiate a jungle or the use of a torch.

I had planned with one of my younger cousins to sneak out one night to carry out the task of chopping this Silk Cotton tree. We were both very excited about the absurd prospect of chopping this Silk Cotton tree to see if it really oozed blood. Armed with cutlass, torch and an alarm clock, my cousin and I set out to the Silk Cotton tree in the dead of night while the rest of the family sat in front of the television watching a horror series, *Dark Shadows*.

In the glow of the faint moonlight, I could see this magnificent tree standing above all else in the bushy valley. As we neared the tree, my cousin heard the cry of a barn owl high above us, scaring the life out this little brute. He dropped the torch racing home in the darkness, leaving me behind to carry out this task by myself. I had heard the cries of the barn owls before, so it didn't really frighten me. In Trinidad, barn owls are known as 'Jumbie birds' and whenever you heard one cry out at night, there was always the presumption that someone would die. If that was anything to go by, my uncle's mother died a few days later, after a lengthy illness.

The hairs on the back of my neck stood up like miniature soldiers as I neared the Silk Cotton tree. I used the cutlass to clear a path to the tree trunk. Holding the clock in one hand

and the cutlass in the other, I waited for the clock to alarm. Across the river, a cow in its pen bellowed the loudest moo from a cow I had ever heard. I held on to the clock and cutlass, almost wetting myself with fright. Soon, I regained my composure and waited for the clock to alarm. There was an eerie tension and silence. I heard voices coming from the stream, or so I thought. My feet kept telling me *run*, but my willpower - or maybe fright - kept me rooted to the spot, cutlass raised, poised for the chop.

If anyone remembers those old-time alarm clocks with the two bells at the top, then you would know what a cacophonous sound it made when alarming. The sound was enough to wake the dead. The bells on the clock echoed through the emptiness of the night making it sound louder than it really was. I looked up at the majestic tree and started to hack away at it with much enthusiasm. I shone the torch on the butchered spot on the tree trunk. An opaque sap oozed from where the blade ravaged the bark. The cow mooed again; I paid no attention to it this time. Overhead, high in the Silk Cotton tree, an owl hooted. I trained the torch on the trunk of the Silk Cotton tree again, still there was no blood. Disappointment anguished me. I started hacking at the tree again, hoping the second assault might produce the desired result. The Silk Cotton tree refused yet again to give up its blood. The owl hooted again; the bamboo clusters rustled in the light wind. I gathered my implements and walked home dejected. *Dark Shadows* still had everyone glued to the television and I quietly retired to my bed unnoticed.

A few years later, when I returned to Arima to live, I managed to fulfil my adventure with the original Silk Cotton tree. This was a much bigger tree with some menacing looking thorns on the trunk. Again, despite some heavy blows with an axe, the tree failed to produce any blood. To be honest, I wasn't hopeful of extracting any blood from the tree. This episode was merely to finally satisfy my curiosity and to put forward any argument that Silk Cotton trees produced blood when chopped at midnight or, any given time of the day or night.

Visiting the Spanish islands of Gran Canarias on a family holiday some decades later, we happened to picnic under a Silk Cotton tree in the mountains. This Silk Cotton tree was significantly smaller than the other two back home in Trinidad. However, this tree got its revenge for the bizarre attacks I had executed on its two larger cousins. I tried to break off one of the thorns from the trunk as a souvenir, my fingers slipped: the thorn punctured my finger drawing blood. This episode proved to be the only time that I witnessed a Silk Cotton tree yield blood.

Douen

Douen

Where did the folklore of Douens originate? Most of our folklores in Trinidad and Tobago seem to have derived from African traditions. It is said that during the 1850s the British carried out a series of blockades against slave ships in the Atlantic. During this time Portuguese ships carrying African slaves bound for Brazil were intercepted by the British and taken to Trinidad as free slaves. The accounts of these slave ships events and their cargo are well documented in Trinidad and Tobago's history.

It is believed the Africans brought with them a tradition that when a child dies before being baptised, they became a sort of living dead, stuck in purgatory. At the time, there was an outbreak of cholera in Trinidad that claimed the lives of many young children as a result. While these folklores have strong African ties, there is a belief that the Douen we refer to in Trinidad originated in Mayan folklore. It is not certain how factual this is, but because of the cultural myriad of the Caribbean, the African traditions are also interwoven with Spanish, French as well as some indigenous influences from the Arawak and the Kalinago tribes.

The stories of Douens had always fascinated me. I was intrigued and yearned to cast my eyes on these human-like creatures with feet and knees facing backwards, faceless with large wide hats on their heads. Folklore has it that Douens are the spirits of unbaptised children who died. The souls of these unbaptised children would roam the woods, frolicking merrily near rivers and streams in jovial folly. These playful noises would have been the attraction that young children followed before being lured away by Douens, never to be seen again.

My mother was always warning me about avoiding certain places where Douens regularly frequented. She gave out this information as if she had expert knowledge of where Douens congregated. Although she tried to instil fear into me, it never did have the effect she tried to convey. The more she endeavoured, the more driven I became to exploring and investigating the whereabouts of these faceless midgets. I vaguely remembered my mother saying that she had seen a Douen while she was, as a young girl washing clothes, in a nearby river where she grew up. My mother was very private, seldom speaking about her childhood. As a boy, and through my adult years, I tried to pry into her early life to understand more about her childhood. She would give you snippets of her childhood, but never enough to put an entire picture together. So, you were always left wondering what her life was really like as a child.

I was competent at truancy, always using a school day to go Jumbie exploring. The price was a painful one to pay, especially when I was punished both at home by my mother and at school by the headmaster. Nevertheless, it was a price I was prepared to pay in my quest to finding these Douens.

There was one riverside where a lot of Douen stories seemed to be originating from. According to several adults, including my own mother, Douens had lured children away from this riverside on numerous occasions. There was one peculiar thing that bothered me about these disappearing children. It seemed very strange that so many young children were being lured away by Douens, yet all the children I knew in my circle could always be accounted for. They were always at school, at least when I attended. However, in those days, it was unheard of to doubt or challenge your parents when they told you something. To challenge your parent's authority would be met with a severe caning, or at least a punishment of some kind.

Using a school day was far easier than having to sneak out in the night to brave the darkness with the threat of snakes as well as other night creatures that roam the forest floor. Also, curiously, I never heard stories of Douens being out at night. Their roving times seem to be centred around mid-day and at dusk, coinciding with when children frolicked without care.

Getting to this river was not an easy task as I had first envisaged. The route which I ventured was chosen purely for concealment. If the neighbours or anyone who knew my mother spotted me, it would surely get back to her, and that meant paying the consequences. The route there meant I had to meander my way through huge thickets of what is commonly known as elephant grass. This robust plant grew like sugarcane with leafy blades that cut you like a razor. Having negotiated the jungle of elephant grass, I had to cross an orange orchard as well. This orange estate belonged to a local pharmacist who had some fierce dogs that patrolled the orchard, or so I was told. Reaching the orchard, I paused to sample some of the sweet succulent oranges that hung from the low branches, freely on offer. After having my fill of oranges, I used my T shirt as a bag to stock up on some supplies for later. In the distance the dogs could be heard barking, but they seemed too far away to pose any real threat.

The river wasn't far away now but having filled my stomach with oranges, it made me lethargic, I carried on regardless. There was a clearing leading towards the river. I followed it and a chill went through me like a knife. It was the first time I recalled ever being truly afraid. The voices of young children playing reach my ears. These were the folklore tell-tale signs, signalling the presence of Douens.

I tried to recite a prayer that my mother had taught me. She said I should say it three times over if ever I was afraid or came upon demons. All that came out of my mouth were the words "Our father... our father..." for the life of me, the rest of the prayer could not find its way to my lips. I thought there was nothing now to protect me from these evil midgets that lay ahead. Tracing my way back was not even a viable option at this point, I had to consider the dogs, plus the whole purpose of being here was to find Douens. Turning back was not an option.

I was rooted to the spot for what may have been seconds, but it felt like an eternity to me. Behind me, I could hear the barking dogs getting closer, not realising that I had gotten closer to the dwellings. The children's voices grew louder, and their frolicking appeared more jovial. With a brave premonition, I proceeded with some measure of caution, moving stealthily along the riverbank.

From my vantage point, looking down into the river, I recognised some of the boys who attended another primary school. They were splashing about in the shallow water, pelting each other with half eaten oranges and swinging like Tarzan, from a thick vine that hung loosely from the overhanging trees. I looked around trying to see if anyone was wearing wide brim hats or had reversed feet, I saw none. Fear averted; I was relieved, but disappointed that they were not Douens. I wasted no time in joining the fun. But as the adage goes, 'after joy comes sorrow' and again, my reward was a multitude of vexed blows from my mother with the thick leather belt.

At school, I overheard some children saying that there were Douens at another river. So, not satisfied with my first endeavour, I sought to investigate this new rendezvous for Douens. The search proved futile; as all that was found there were remnants of empty biscuit packets, soft drink bottles, and the remains of a makeshift fire where someone had cooked a meal. Whoever had cooked here, left discarded paper plates scattered recklessly on the banks of the river. There were bits of chicken and other animal bones littered about too. I decided then to embark on one final search to satisfy my curiosity before abandoning the challenge of ever finding a Douen that day. Despite my best efforts, not a single clue to indicate that there were Douens about could be found.

Judging from the two previous occasions to find Douens, I ventured out of my comfort zone to a river in D'abadie. A friend of the family visiting one day was relating to my mother that two children from a district called Five Rivers were almost lured away by Douens. Luckily for the children, they were spotted by a local gardener who recognised that the children were being led away. He reportedly chased after the Douens, saving the children from coming to harm or being led away, never to be seen again.

I listened attentively from the adjacent room gathering as much information as I could muster for the location of the river. I knew it could only be one river they were referring to. If you were travelling along the main road westwards, you passed over the river on a huge iron bridge. The river was about two hundred feet under the bridge, the water crystal clear with tall verdant clusters of bamboo hanging over, creating a canopy. On one side of the riverbank was a lovely house on flat ground, with a rich green sprawling lawn. There was also a corral with a white wooden fence, where several thoroughbred stallions grazed happily. As a young boy, I had dreamt of living on a place like that: there was a romantic aura to the property. In the garden were beautiful flowerbeds and various fruit trees, all in abundance with colourful crop.

Truancy played a key role in this adventure. To access this river required a bus journey. The consequences of this journey also had grave implications on my return. So, to avoid the leather belt, I manipulated the outing so I would get back before my mother returned home from work that day. In those days, I had no watch, so I had to judge the time by averaging or taking note of the sun's position in the sky. This was a common way of keeping track of the time when your parents gave you a curfew. In those days, wristwatches were a luxury, even for the richer kids. You judged the time by knowledge that when the sun was directly overhead it was mid-day, and once your shadow started to lengthen behind you then evening was closing in.

The adventure, like the previous ones, proved once again to be fruitless. There were no signs of Douens, just an elderly Indian man fetching water from the river to irrigate the various crops of tomatoes, lettuce, cucumbers, and peppers he had cultivated not far from the riverbank. I watched the man go about his chores as I continued along the river searching for signs of Douens. After a futile search of the areas with little basins adequate for swimming, I found nothing. I abandoned the quest and made my way home in good time. My mother was none the wiser if I had attended school or not. I was pleased with myself to have outsmarted her on this occasion.

It transpired that the man tending to his crops knew my mother well. Some weeks later, he must have met her during Saturday market shopping. I did not escape the flogging; the leather strap and I were reunited once again. My mother had this uncanny knack of always learning of my truancy and my escapades from school. Little escaped this acute and clever woman. My mother had no formal education, but she was able to correct and assist me with my reading and teaching me to count. Once, while she was listening to me read *Fluff and Nip*, I inserted a few lines into the story as I read. She smacked me behind the head asking. 'Yuh think I dotish?' No matter what subterfuge I employed, my mother always found out what I had been up to, even if it took several weeks or months.

I was quite satisfied with myself that the existence of Douens was a myth, a folklore as it stands. Just like the Silk Cotton tree was an apparent fabrication by some clever soul to discourage young children from playing near these supposedly demonic trees. Maybe people never saw Douens, instead they must have heard truant boys frolicking near rivers or streams which led them to assume it was Douens. Many years later, in my teens someone said they saw a Douen near a river, a few miles from where I lived. This time I adopted another approach. I climbed a tall tree near to the area described by my friend and waited…and waited…and waited. No Douens arrived. I had been on the tree so long, cramp began to set in. The cramp was so bad causing me to almost fall off the tree as I descended.

As dusk began to paint a vibrant hue in the sky. The kind of picturesque scenes you saw in the movies. I ambled along the river in a slow walk home hoping that I may still encounter a Douen or two. Darkness crept in quickly, ending my search for these elusive Douens. These little frolicking faceless midgets managed to elude me on every occasion. I was beginning to think these little demons were afraid of me. Maybe I was carrying around too many Jumbie protection that kept them away? I will never know, as I never again attempted to seek out the existence of Douens, closing the chapter on the faceless midgets trapped in purgatory.

Largahoo

Largahoo

Satisfied that I could not find any Douens, based on my investigative haunts, I shifted my attention to finding a Largahoo. Now, this would prove much more difficult than finding Douens. A Largahoo, according to folklore, was a man who changed into half beast, half human, who dragged heavy chains and a coffin with him. He retained the torso of a human but had the head of an animal - namely a dog, horse, or mule. The name Largahoo derives from the French word 'loup garou' meaning werewolf. I had heard many stories of people who had encountered these shape-shifting demons. No Largahoo story was ever the same. Some claimed it was like a big dog, others a horse, some a donkey but one thing that was of relative consistency, he was always dragging chains.

In the days when we had no electricity and sometime after my stepfather had died, my mother claimed to have seen a Largahoo. My mother was the bread winner of the home now. With three young children to look after, she laboured by day to earn a living. By night she laboured with the household chores to ensure we were fed and had clean clothes to wear. She would do all her washing at night. Being out all day working, it was the only time she could set aside to complete this chore. Once she had prepared our meals and did our lunches for the following day, she concentrated on getting the laundry done. Some nights, she would leave the washing, claiming that a Largahoo was staring at her from the darkness, growling with fiery eyes. She said, all that was visible was the head and glowing eyes, with a menacing snarl.

One night, my mother asked me to wait up with her so she could do the washing. My mother was no coward, so this thing must have really frightened her if she had to ask for company. It must have been just after nine o'clock when she started to do her washing. That night, I armed myself with a slingshot I had made for hunting birds, and some well-rounded pebbles, large enough to inflict pain on any living target. I was a good shot too, seldom missing a target.

Armed with my weapon, ammunition, and a strong cup of black coffee that my mother had prepared. I sat on the wooden steps and watched my mother as she soaped and scrubbed away at the pile of dirty laundry. At punctuated intervals she would slap her legs where mosquitoes were attacking her. She paused with a curious gaze as she held up the flambeau for better illumination. Casting a curious look my way, she set down the light and continued washing.

A few moments later, she held up the flambeau again, this time in a whisper she said. "It's there, I can see the eyes". My mother lifted the flambeau higher. I could see nothing in the darkness but there was fear in my mother's face that I had never seen before, and there was a smell of wet dog. I fired a shot into the darkness, and another. I could hear the pebbles whistle through the bushes, and I doubted whether I hit anything. There was a little thump and a rustling in the dark. I fired two more shots into the eerie night; this time, I was certain I struck something. I waited, but there was no movement in the darkness. My mother held up the flambeau beckoning me back as I made my way into the darkness. After a few moments, nothing moved in the bushes. She called me back with an urgency in her voice and abandoned the washing that night. Since that encounter, I never recalled my mother washing under the cover of darkness again.

They say to kill a Largahoo required great skill. According to folklore tales, to kill this beast, you had to beat it with a stick that had been anointed with concoction of holy oils and holy water and left to soak for nine days. I had no intentions of killing this demonic beast. My only ambition was to find one, look it in the eyes and be contented that I had found a Largahoo. This, so far, had proven to be a challenge, in more ways than one. Then one day, my luck changed.

Rumours were flying about that a certain man in the neighbourhood was a Largahoo. This frail looking man had a hunched back with two teeth in his mouth. One on the upper jaw and the other on the lower jaw. He lived on his own in a very creepy looking wooden house set on concrete pillars, with an overgrown garden. An ideal setting for Largahoo, according to Largahoo experts. From my own memory, I can't ever remember seeing the house illuminated at night. This made me even more suspicious that a Largahoo could be residing there. I began to gather thoughts that this Largahoo hunt was starting to look very promising indeed.

Catching sight of a Largahoo would prove to be far more complicated than anticipated. To begin with, timing had to be crucial to witness a Largahoo in transformation from human to beast. Some accounts about Largahoo was, fractured if not conflicting. People said that the Largahoo changed from human to beast around midnight. However, many people who had related stories of Largahoo sightings had mentioned times earlier than midnight. I concluded people just associated supernatural things to occur at midnight, a time generally associated with being the ungodly hour.

To witness the transformation of a Largahoo was going to present more challenges than I previously imagined. There was only one feasible way this could be achieved, in my opinion. I would have to sneak into the house where a suspected Largahoo lived, conceal myself in a vantage position and await the transformation. Somehow, I couldn't envisage myself being that person. Brave as I was, it was something not even worth contemplating at this stage.

This old man had a huge mango tree in his yard. The mango tree would provide a good view into his house as well as camouflaging me in the night since his property wasn't adequately illuminated. The absence of light in the house also provided additional challenges. It would be near impossible to see the transformation of this Largahoo from the confines of the mango tree into a darkened room. I resigned myself to the fact that witnessing a transformation was totally impossible, just getting a glimpse would suffice. Witnessing the Largahoo emerging from the house on its way to haunt the living would be spectacular enough to satisfy my eager curiosity.

Speculation arose too: how did this transformation from man to beast took place? In my head, it was difficult to visualise the entire process from man to Largahoo. I could only assume from watching werewolf movies how this manifestation may transpire. Sometimes I would prompt my mother to narrate Largahoo stories in the hope of gaining more knowledge on this beast. My mother always referred to those nights when she saw a Largahoo in the yard. It was her only experience of any Largahoo. The odd thing was, there was a recollection of my stepfather reporting to my mother one night, there was a man on a horse in the far end of the garden watching him. My stepfather would stay up late at night crafting jewellery which he sold to a retail outlet in Port of Spain. The neighbour's husband had also recalled seeing a man on a horse in the early hours of the morning. He described this man as dressed in white with a cork hat and sitting on a majestic grey horse.

Now, the old man who I thought was a good Largahoo prospect faced a barrage of abuse from many school children, me included. We would pelt stones or half eaten mangoes at his house. One day I scattered salt near his front gate. It was rumoured that if there was salt on the ground a Largahoo couldn't cross it. That never worked for on many occasions he would come out of the house, hunched over, walking stick in hand, cursing at us in the most profane way as we scampered away in laughter. This man became the target for my first Largahoo scrutiny. I was buzzing with excitement with the thought catching glimpse of a Largahoo as he emerged from his house.

My mother had all these remedies for scaring away demons and evil spirits. Her most prized was the Lord's Prayer. She also had these words which she uttered in Sanskrit or Urdu that I could never pronounce. Sometimes when I was frightened at night, she would put garlic around the bed and a crucifix on a beaded chain under my pillow to ward off any evil spirits. On my sisters she pinned a small leather pouch, which she got from a pundit. To this day, I never learnt what it contained, but almost all Indian babies had one, as well as a jet bracelet. My mother would also perform this process she called *jharay*. This involved putting garlic and onion skins along with seven small chilli peppers and salt in a small brown paper bag. She recited a prayer making circles around you seven times. Once this was finished, she burnt the bag in the garden.

If these defences were good enough for my mother to ward off evil spirits, then there was no reason why they would not work for me as well. I decided these were the armour necessary for protecting me from any Largahoo that I may encounter in my search. If this demon beast was capable of shapeshifting into various types of animals, then some form of serious protection was required.

Planning these Jumbie expeditions had to be quite discreet and required much subterfuge. If my mother got wise about my antics, there would be a permanent attachment with the dreaded leather belt. Earlier in the day, preparation for Largahoo defence began. Selecting some cloves of garlic and wrapping them in a small rag, along with the crucifix I pinched from my mother's jewellery box. I concealed the arsenal of garlic, crucifix, and penknife under a bucket in the yard.

The anticipation of nightfall was overwhelming. I had to contain my excitement with great difficulty. During the day I was super-efficient too, completing all my chores to impeccable standards so not to anger my mother. I did not want to give her any cause for retrieving that leather belt.

As the twilight descended, there was a chill in the air, before long, torrential rain began to quench the thirst of the dry earth. Listening to the heavy rain pounding on the iron roof, beating out a sultry rhythm. I watched my mother scamper about to place a bucket and a large bowl to collect water in the two places where the roof leaked. Opening a window, I watched the raindrops as they landed on the banana leaves making them dance. The chickens on the orange tree didn't seem to mind the rain at all. As darkness fell, I closed the window and folded my arms around my knees, sitting on the chair feeling disappointed. Suddenly, I remembered the crucifix. Making a quick dash outside, I retrieved my mother's prized crucifix and my penknife before it got washed away when the yard flooded.

I opened the window and watched as the water level rose in the yard. The rain continued in its torrent as my mother mended a skirt for work the next day. Largahoo hunting for me that night had to be abandoned. Soon, I was curled up in bed after a delightful cup of hot chocolate, sweetened with condensed milk and dusted with a sprinkling of cinnamon and nutmeg. I never saw my mother finish darning her skirt. And for that night, Largahoo had escaped.

Some weeks later, before I could execute another plan of Largahoo spotting, the old man died, alone in the house. It was a very disappointing turn of events. Why did he have to die? I asked myself, almost expecting an answer. He had been dead for almost three days, before being discovered by an inquisitive neighbour. There was gossip rallying around that animal bones and skins were found in the house. I don't know how true it was, but I heard too that a human skull was found in the house.

After his death and the funeral had taken place, there was a light in the house every night. It was rumoured that he had come back to haunt the house to prevent his family from occupying the property. This man had no visitors, he lived alone, yet he had one of the largest funerals in the area that I can recall. It was mentioned that he came from some bigshot background in Woodbrook and was related to some famous painter.

It had taken a few years, I was well into in my teens then, when the chance to engage in some Largahoo investigation happened. Though, by now the belief that Largahoo existed was lost. However, there was my curiosity yet to be satisfied. I was older now, braver, and more ambitious in adventuring. Again, going on what I was hearing. A Largahoo was reportedly sighted in Wallerfield, an area located east of Arima. It used to be the site of the old American Army airfield, during World War II and known locally as 'the base.' There were two huge stone pillars on both sides of the road that was once the checkpoint for entering the military complex. Today they still stand as sentinels and reminders of the war initiative and the American presence on the island.

After the war ended and the Americans abandoned the complex, returning to their native land. The area was now saturated with agricultural farming. Houses along the road were few and far between, depending on the acreage of the farms. Most of the old airfield and its abandoned structures was overgrown with bushes. It was also polluted with all manner of refuse, including derelict vehicles, building waste, and even dead animals. The wide roads were sparsely lit by streetlamps. If you lived in this area and didn't own a car, you had to ensure that you got the last taxi around ten o'clock. If for whatever reason you missed the last taxi, walking was the only option for the five-mile journey, depending on how far into Wallerfield you lived. Worse yet, you had to cross a bridge called 'Jumbie Bridge', so named because people attested to seeing spirits near or on the bridge. Sometimes the spirits were blamed for the numerous and sometimes fatal motor accidents that occurred on or near the bridge. The river that ran there had some decent swimming basins but with increased pig farming, local people avoided swimming there.

I surveyed the area during the daytime where the Largahoo was apparently spotted by a farmer on his way home. The farmer, who was returning home late one night after a few drinks at a bar near the main junction, related to his friend that on seeing the Largahoo – standing majestic like Hercules, with chains wrapped across his body. He was so fear-stricken, the farmer closed his eyes and began running all the way to his house. He lamented about his horror and was unsure on how he knew when he had reached his house without opening his eyes.

Surveying the area was crucial to ensure I had good access to open road. If the worst was to happen. I could easily make a run for it if Mr Largahoo decided to chase me. This time there was no house to stakeout. I was at the mercy of this expanse of abandoned military airfield and open to the elements. The abandoned airfield was also a haven for a variety of other pursuits. Lovers used the desolate airfield as a love nest, young restless drivers wanting to take advantage of the paved areas to engage in illegal drag racing tournaments, and car thieves capitalised on the many secluded hideouts the abandoned airfield provided. It made a good cover facility for these car thieves to strip stolen vehicles down to a shell.

Armed with a six-cell battery flashlight, cloves of garlic and my mother's crucifix for protection, I headed out to Largahoo land. I stopped for a brief period where the farmer had seen the Largahoo. Like some sort of séance ritual, I stood there hoping for a sign or connection to this Largahoo. Having already secured a vantage position to await this Largahoo, I made myself comfortable. I had found a sheltered area to protect me from the elements as I waited patiently for an appearance of Mister Largahoo. I made sure to take along some food in preparation for a long night. The night was indeed long, cold, damp, and reeked of pig shit; something I did not cater for. I shivered through the night trying to keep awake, warm, and alert. I struggled to keep my T shirt over my nose to block out the stench of the pig shit from the nearby farms. Throughout the night, the silence was punctuated with the sound of a motor vehicles on the road. I couldn't tell whether the vehicles were heading to the country or into Arima. Other times I could hear the roar of the car engines in the distance. I could tell it was drag racing somewhere in the disused airfield.

At some point during the cold night, I had fallen asleep only to be awaken by the sounds of roosters from the nearby farms, signalling that a new day was approaching. I felt a surge of disappointment rush through as I shivered in the cold, dew-soaked morning. As the sun rose, there was little else to do but make my way towards the main road. From there it was possible to hitch a ride back into Arima, none-the-wiser if Largahoo existed or not. I was furious with myself for falling asleep. Who knows, the Largahoo may have made an appearance while I slept. The only saving grace now was I no longer had to fear an appointment with the leather belt.

I had forsaken the lure of Largahoo hunting until I went to spend a weekend with relatives in Champ Fleur, home of the country's first brewing company, Carib. My relatives lived high in the mountains, where little pockets of houses dotted the hillsides, surrounded by lush greenery. Some of these houses cling precariously on the edge of cliffs, held in place by wooden stilts that appeared fragile to the eye. Others were built on more solid concrete foundations making them structurally secure on the dangerous slopes. It held my fascination how people got building materials to these locations since there were no clear roads leading to these dwellings. Most of the access to these houses were via steps cut into the earth and held into shape by steel plates or timber. It must have been a laborious task getting steel, bricks, cement, timber, sand, and water to these sites in preparation for constructing these elaborate houses.

The house of my relatives was perched on a steep slope overlooking a deep gorge with a river below. It stood on solid concrete pillars, with a concrete stairwell leading directly into the living area. It had five bedrooms and one of the largest kitchens I have ever seen in a house anywhere. I am not exaggerating when I say you played tennis in the living room area. I shudder to think of the amount of manual labour that was required for getting building materials to the site.

The water in the river below was a muddy brown from days of heavy rainfall. In some places you could see exposed soil on the slopes from where the earth had eroded due the heavy rains. Tree roots were left exposed as they hung dangerously on the slopes. Sometimes only tangled thick vines prevented them from tumbling down into the river below. It was an eerie feeling looking over the low wall from the veranda into the deep gorge below. The surrounding land around the house was cultivated with oranges, limes, breadfruit, and mango trees. Nearer the house there were huge clusters of lemongrass and sugar cane patches along with several rows scotch bonnet pepper trees laden with red, green, and yellow crop. Under the house was several hessian sacks filled with peppers ready to be taken to the market where they would fetch a fair price. My relatives knew about diversifying. In the dry months the focus was on basket weaving and in the wet season they cultivated crops such as peppers and limes that earned them a good living.

The first night with my relatives, it was folklore tales galore. One of my aunts, who was also visiting, loved to narrate a good story, almost as eloquently as my mum. It always amazed me how she wove these stories, and it was never the same story twice. As we all sat in the living room that first night drinking whiskey and coconut water, she announced randomly, "Largahoo attacked a man causing him to fall into the gorge". She said this with so much emotion, you would have thought she knew this gentleman well. The man had suffered a broken arm, ankle as well as several huge gashes about his body. My aunt explained he had a miraculous escape from death. The river was swollen with a ferocious current from heavy rainfall earlier that day. Trees on the riverbank created a safety net, preventing the man from falling into the river and being swept away by the raging waters.

He was found unconscious the following day and taken to hospital. Upon recovering, he revealed a Largahoo had attacked him on his way home. Running to escape the shapeshifting demon, he slipped, falling down the slippery slopes. He recalled the last thing he saw was the Largahoo at the top of the hill, laughing and shaking huge chains, with a huge box on his back and a bright moon behind him. I sat listening, half doubting and half wanting to believe this man. They could not associate him with being drunk as it was established, he was not a consumer of alcohol.

Up in the hills lent an eerie aura as darkness crept in. During the daytime, views of the mountains and the valley was exceptionally beautiful. Dotted with yellow hues from the Poui and Immortelle trees, clouds kissing the high mountain peaks. The scenery was postcard perfect with varying shades of green mingling with the hues of the hills.

Songbirds chorused across the lush green mountains with a beautiful zephyr blowing over your face and the air so pure you felt renewed with every breath. By night, it was a different orchestra. Weird sounds bellowed from the depths of the gorge and high into the hills. Although I wasn't scared, it sent some shivers down my spine. Cicadas, night birds, frogs and who knows what else was responsible for creating this nocturnal opera that began with the arrival of darkness. For some odd reason, after midnight this operatic cacophony would cease and plunge the mountain into silence, punctuated only by the occasional haunting screech from some nocturnal creature.

The next day I scouted the area my relatives identified where the man had fallen. It was a truly a miracle indeed how this man survived such a fall without sustaining more serious injuries and without dying. He had fallen almost five hundred feet down the slope across the steep face with huge, exposed boulders, limestone shards and tree stumps jutting out of the red earth. It was a revelation too, when, one relative revealed a sound suspicion of who the Largahoo might be. This invigorated my inquisitive nature even further.

The man suspected of being the Largahoo was a short, stocky man with a muscular build. He could well have been in his sixties with well-toned muscles, short greying hair and a scraggy beard, matching the colour of his hair. He lived alone in his quaint little blue house that stood on concrete pillars about four feet off the ground. The steps that led to the entrance of the house were lined with potted plants, all blooming in vibrant colours. The yard was pristine and dotted with beautifully kept flowerbeds along the fence edges. At the four corners of the yard were tall bamboo poles with different coloured flags fluttering in the light breeze. The flags resembled those used by Hindus when they had their *pujas*. Local people held a strong belief that this man was an obeahman. Visitors came there from all corners of the country seeking his services in witchcraft and Obeah. In my limited experience, I had seen homes where people who were believed to be Obeah practitioners lived. This house had some tell-tale signs that suggested this man could in fact be an obeahman, but a Largahoo? I needed to have proof. And so, the process of seeking out a Largahoo began all over again.

Champ Fleur was an area that wasn't really known to me. I had been there a few times as a young boy but all I remembered was swimming in the river. So, as not to arouse any suspicions with my relatives, I kept my intentions to myself. Had I enlightened them of my pursuits, they may have discouraged my actions. A week or so later, I returned to the area to surreptitiously carry out reconnaissance without the knowledge of my relatives. This reconnaissance was necessary, the last thing I wanted was someone spotting me in the middle of the night, mistakenly thinking I was a prowling thief.

The Obeahman's house was adjacent to a vacant plot of land. This was perfect to camouflage me as I undertook my Largahoo mission. The land was overgrown with vines, tall bushes, trees, and elephant grass. The trees were strong and tall enough for me to climb with good solid branches to support my weight. I made sure to secure a clear track through the dense vines and grass to a selected tree where I could perch. From here, I could get a good vantage of the front gate, the side, and the back of the house. I checked the tree to ensure there were no wasp nests: the last thing you want is to be attacked by wasps after disturbing their nest.

A friend of mine father owned a pair of binoculars, which he used whenever he attended horse racing at Santa Rosa Park. I coerced my friend into stealing the binoculars so I could borrow it for my mission. He was apprehensive at first to perform a dishonest act. Eventually, he went against all his moral principles and got me the binoculars. I was thankful, rewarding him with the gratitude of six Julie mangoes that I liberated from a tree belonging to one of the posh residences on the other side of the village from where we lived. A place called Christina Gardens, where some years earlier was the scene of a brutal murder that rocked the country. The murder of this British socialite had attracted worldwide attention. The murdered woman's body was buried in a shallow grave, with lettuce planted on it to disguise the burial. The killer was eventually caught in Guyana and brought back to Trinidad where he was tried, convicted, and hanged.

On the night that I chose to stake out this alleged Largahoo home, there was a hive of activity taking place at the house. People were in and out of the yard at regular intervals. Candles were lit in the yard and at the back of the house there was a small bonfire. I began to have second thoughts about the stakeout when suddenly, there was a melodious chanting of hymns. I had trouble focussing the binoculars in the dark and simultaneously balancing on the tree, to get a good view of what was taking place.

What I saw really did surprise me. Here was one of my relatives dancing about in the yard with a goat wrapped over his shoulders. This shocked me more than anything else, given that he was the one who claimed this man was a Largahoo. A ferocious rapture of drumming began, I could feel the rhythm of the drums inside my chest. The beat of the drums was so intoxicating, you felt you could fly. I kept my arms firmly wrapped around the branch trying to focus the binoculars. I noticed the Obeahman with a cutlass in his hand, his head tied with a blue sash. He was rocking, making a circular motion, and skanking like a Rastafarian dancing to a dub rhythm.

The beat of the drums intensified, so did the dancing of those gathered in the yard. The rhythms of the drums continued; the chorus of voices continued to chant hymns. Some of them I knew and was tempted to hum along. This went on for about another ten minutes. The Obeahman lifted the goat's head, in a single motion with the cutlass, he had the goat's head in one hand, and the cutlass in the other. Blood dripped from the cutlass as he lifted the head into the air and chanted. Someone appeared to be collecting the blood from the cadaver in a calabash bowl as it bled out. The singing became a sombre wail. Suddenly, amidst the chanting and the drumming, someone was aiming a flashlight with a purposeful search on the empty plot. I sat motionless on the tree, hiding the binoculars to prevent any reflection. The beam of light traced across the bushes, up the trees, repeating the process several times. All the while the hymns and drumming continued with renewed tempo.

I dared not move as I waited patiently, motionless and in complete silence. I could have sworn I wasn't even breathing air as I kept still. More people arrived and joined the peculiar ritual as it progressed. I clung to the tree for dear life wondering if they had spotted me. The flashlight search began again. Now there were two beams cutting through the darkness. After a few minutes, the searching beams disappeared. Just to be sure I waited a while longer. Clambering down the tree in quiet stealth, inching my way through the thick bushes and unto the road. Casting a fleeting glance behind me to make sure no one had seen me. I started the long walk back to the main road. Here, I waited for a taxi and breathed a sigh of relief once I sat safely in the cab.

My decision to abandon the stakeout wasn't an easy one. But I had feared anytime soon, those inquisitive beams from the torches would venture over to the plot to make further investigations. Maybe the Obeahman had an inclination someone was watching him. If that had been the case, I did not want to end up like the goat. The safest and most practical thing to do was to get myself to safer ground and away from the macabre ritual I had just witnessed. As the taxi maintained a steady pace along the main road, the driver looked at me through the rear-view mirror and said, "Dis place have real Obeah oui!". I was about to ask what he meant when he proceeded to explain, "I just pass ah woman in the Croisée, a lighted candle in she mouth, ringing ah bell and sprinkling *Ixor*a water in de road. Imagine at this hour of the night, carrying on with dis arseness". Nothing more was said in the taxi. I alighted in Arima and walked home.

This renewed setback in my search to find a Largahoo was beginning to make me a little bit despondent. Having come so close yet allowing it to slip through my fingers. I consoled myself with the thought that it was best to abandon the mission, rather than end up in a shallow grave somewhere, like that British socialite. I was happy to finally be in the comfort of my bed and cast the entire Largahoo episode behind me.

A few months after the incident, and now distant in my memory, I had a shocking discovery. I met my relative in Port of Spain, the one that was dancing with the goat on his shoulders. He enlightened me that he had attended a Shango ritual at the Obeahman house. He said the Obeahman confessed that he was sure someone was watching them. I learnt too; the event was a Shango sacrifice. I didn't let up that it was me in the adjacent plot looking on, although I was very tempted to confess. The intricacies of how my relative came to be there on the night, remains a mystery. I never pursued any conversation to find out more about his involvement with this Obeahman.

I never did really understand much about this Shango ritual until much later in my adult years when I was privileged to be at one of these rituals quite by chance. I was at a bar one Friday afternoon drinking when, suddenly the roaring rhythm of drums filled the air. I saw, on the main road, a procession numbering about thirty, chanting and following a man with a goat over his shoulders. Leading the procession was another man, dancing with a machete, his head tied with a red sash. Curiosity got the better of me and I left my beer on the counter and followed the procession.

They danced, chanted, and drummed along the road, turning into a side street and then into a yard. I didn't see it but next thing I knew, the goat had no head. I recognised a few people in the congregation and none of them questioned my presence. I watched them as two men began to skin the goat. A shower of rain tumbled down, and I raced back to the bar and the comfort of a couple more beers.

Shango worship and ritual traditions came from Nigeria, where Shango is the god of thunder and practiced mostly among those of Yoruba traditions in Trinidad and Tobago. These sacrifices performed by Shango worshippers were done to please the gods. The rituals meant that a link could be maintained between mankind and the gods. A connection between the material world, *aiyé* and the supernatural, *orun*. The sacrifice pleased the Orisha gods and allowed life and harmony to prevail. One thing I did notice at the ritual was the numerous amounts of apples, grapes, corn, and yam placed near a small shrine in the yard. Similar rituals exist in the Hindu religion with sacrifices made to the god Kali.

I wasn't convinced that the Obeahman in Champ Fleur was a Largahoo. Throughout all the stories, I had never heard over the years of any Obeahmen transforming into a Largahoo. Even more confusion existed as to how one could transform themselves into a Largahoo? None of these questions ever became lucid to me as did my investigations to find a Largahoo. Following many trails, none prevailed with even a glimmer of hope of finding this elusive beast of the night. Eventually, with some reluctance, the only option now was to give up on this absurd notion of finding a Largahoo.

Just as my disappointing efforts was beginning to bear down on me, I had reached a decision to abandon all endeavours to finding a Largahoo, something happened. Overhearing a peculiar conversation in the bar where I worked, someone had come face to face with a Largahoo. This young man claimed that the Largahoo was just sitting on a bridge, but it never bothered him. What I gleaned from my eavesdropping, the Largahoo was just sitting on this bridge. It was odd how the Largahoo never attacked this young man. And what was more peculiar, the young man just walked casually by. The story seemed too far-fetched to warrant any truth from it. Nevertheless, it reignited the inquisitive nature in me to investigate.

One night after a late show at the cinema, I decided to walk in the direction of the haunted bridge. It was a longer route home but spotting a Largahoo took precedence over my journey home. Late shows would normally finish around 12:30 am so that would give this Largahoo ample time to parade the streets, looking for people to haunt. The bridge where the Largahoo was spotted was one, well known to me. This bridge had an eerie aura to it. Crossing it at night you could almost feel as if something would reach out from under the bridge and grab you. The bridge always gave me the creeps, despite my bravery. Even in my adult years, I avoided crossing this bridge at night-time. While crossing the other bridge sent shivers through me, it didn't really scare me, this bridge did. There were always some supernatural stories attached to the bridge, from as far back as I could remember. There was always some tale of evil spirits spotted on or near the bridge. It was the sole reason that I avoided it as a youngster and even as a braver adult.

As a youngster, I attended a kindergarten school not far from the bridge. The teacher was an elderly Indian man with a hunched back. As a young boy, I always associated him with being a Largahoo. Maybe it was his hunched back or, the fact that he had scary bulging eyes, almost as they were falling out of its sockets. As I grew older, I concluded he wasn't capable of being a Largahoo, he was a chronic alcoholic. He was only passionate about two things, educating children and consuming alcohol. I struggled to imagine how parents trusted him with their young children. His proximity to the bridge had made me associate him with evil.

A dense cluster of trees and bamboo weaved a canopy over the river near one side of the bridge and on the other, a thick overgrowth of elephant grass dipped their long blades to the river. On the riverbank was a cultivated plot with oranges, limes, mangoes, and Chinese coconuts. I knew it well, for as a boy I had pilfered many fruits from small orchard. Part of the riverbed had been concreted. Heavy rains and floods had eroded the banks and weakened the original wooden structure.

The concrete riverbed created a cascade, and you could hear the flow of water tipping into the basin below as you passed over the bridge. The river itself stank. People were in the habit of discarding dead animals in the river and the nearby poultry shop deposited its waste as well as domestic rubbish being dumped into the waterway. Despite warning signs posted to prevent the dumping of rubbish, people recklessly ignored these signs and would dump refuse openly, without fear or concern. A practice that was not only illegal, but it was also unsightly and created a huge stink especially when the weather was extremely hot. The neighbourhood stray dogs also dragged rotting meat into the road and sidewalks, adding to the disgust of the practice.

The night I decided to do the Largahoo walk, the late movie was a horror film with Peter Cushing and Cristopher Lee, a Dracula offering. In most of these horror films, Christopher Lee played the Dracula character and Peter Cushing the Dracula slayer. This film however, Peter Cushing was the blood sucking culprit. It was a disappointing movie; Peter Cushing lacks the character to play a vampire, Christopher Lee was the epitome of a Dracula. After the film I walked casually along this dreaded road with heightened anticipation. This bridge had a reputation for Jumbies, and tonight presented promising prospects.

A sudden stab of fear struck me; I had no crucifix or garlic in my pocket, all I had was my trusted penknife that went everywhere with me. I even slept with it under my pillow sometimes. Part of me was urging myself to turn back, but I was determined that if Mister Largahoo was there, I wasn't going to miss him tonight. If there was going to be a revelation, tonight was the night Largahoo, and I will come face to face with each other. It was him or me tonight. Mentally, I was ready for whatever was to befall me that night. I wasn't ready for death, but if it was to be, I was not running away. At least I didn't think so.

It had taken me about ten minutes to walk from Arima to the bridge. One of the good things about this road, there was the ample street lighting on both sides of the road. There were a lot more houses too, only at this time of night they were all in complete darkness. The only movements at this time of night was the light breeze and dogs ambling about in the yards, barking at everything that moved. The bridge itself, had no lighting. Walking along casually, hands in my pocket, one hand clutching the penknife. I came to the summit of a hill that sloped down to the bridge. From this vantage point, I could see a human like figure sitting on the iron rails on the bridge. I became apprehensive, stopping to take the knife out of my pocket. I opened the blade and held the knife inside my pocket with the blade facing up. Walking cautiously, minding every step I took towards the bridge.

Moving closer, the figure just sat there on the iron rails. I must have blinked for a second, when I opened my eyes again, the figure was gone. Nevertheless, I continued walking, exercising extreme caution, my head down but my eyes focused on the bridge. When I looked up again, the figure was there, sitting on the bridge. My heart thumped inside my chest, not that it could thump anywhere else. I felt like it wanted to jump out of my chest to escape, my body rigid as board. I stopped, only to compose myself for a moment. I thought for a moment I was going to wet myself, or worst.

The hairs on the back of my neck stood like needles, the palm of my hands was sweating as I tried to keep a grip on the knife in my pocket. Suddenly, the reality of fear registered within me. Here I was, finally coming face to face with a Largahoo, and I wasn't prepared. I had neglected my armour of garlic cloves and the trusted crucifix. Worst yet, I could not remember any of the prayers or verses my mother had entrusted me with. Could this be the end of me? The thought raced through my mind, but I proceeded, nonetheless for an encounter with Largahoo.

I was holding the knife in my hand, but my fingers kept searching for it in my pocket. My legs became heavy as I got closer and closer to the bridge. The figure sat there unmoving. Fear gripped me; I crossed the road to the other side of the bridge. Now, I heard two voices on the bridge. Suddenly, I was spellbound. I thought, what the hell, two Largahoo together? I was sceptical of moving closer to the bridge. Despite my apprehension to proceed, I kept my strides at a snail's pace, inching my way forward. I could still hear two voices, but only seeing one figure on the bridge. This gave me grave concern, one Largahoo I might be able to deal with, but two? I didn't know what the outcome would be. I was a good runner, and quite prepared to do so if I had too. If nothing scared me before, tonight I was petrified: not of the Largahoo, but of the outcome. There was a strong scent of marijuana in the air as I got closer. I saw the other figure sitting on the ground. As I got nearer, I recognised the figure sitting on the rails. He lived on one of the side streets from the bridge and did a brisk trade peddling marijuana. He recognised me too, and before I could speak, he asked. "Breds, you have a cigarette?". I cannot recall if I answered him or not. I was relieved to have crossed the bridge, but equally disappointed not having seen any Largahoo that night, despite the fright that came over me.

Further along the road, about a mile, I had to cross another bridge. I remembered standing in the middle of the bridge, shouting at the top of my voice. "Come on you fucking Jumbies, come and get me." To this day I don't know what came into my head prompting me to shout out. Just ahead of me stood an old brick factory. I saw what looked like a woman standing at the front the factory. As I got closer, the further away the figure seemed to be. Once I got to the factory I paused, looking around to see where she had disappeared, but saw nothing. I was tempted to walk around the factory to investigate but I was tired and in dire need of my bed.

Once in the comfort of my home, I had a memory jolt, reminding me that people had often spotted spirits lurking around the brick factory. Residents too, often claimed to have seen a woman, some said she appeared to be holding a baby. Maybe she was indeed a *churaille.* There was no history of a woman dying there with a baby, so it was a strange occurrence to the area. Maybe something had happened there long before our time, unknowing to those who lived there. I was glad to be home safely tucked up in my bed after another unfulfilled night of Jumbie hunting. Despite my tiredness, I struggled to sleep that night. Every time I closed my eyes, I was transported back to the days when my mother narrated stories and the fear I had of opening my eyes. Sleep eventually came and consumed me. Before I knew it, day had broken, and the roosters were alert waking the neighbourhood.

I did not expect this, but I heard many tales that there were Largahoo and La Diablesse in Port of Spain. Sightings were especially in the East Dry River and Belmont area, with talk too, about Largahoo near Lapeyrouse cemetery in Woodbrook. I had my doubts about the existence of Largahoo and La Diablesse in Port of Spain, more so because I could not fathom the thought of Jumbies in town. The city was well illuminated with electricity throughout, and I associated places like Belmont and Woodbrook to be inhabited by middle, and upper-class people. There was no way I thought, Largahoo and La Diablesse would be parading the streets of Port of Spain, doing what? But once again, my curiosity compelled me to investigate.

According to whispers, Belmont Valley Road was a haven for Largahoo as well as near Lapeyrouse cemetery in Woodbrook. I really could not allow this opportunity to pass me by without some exploration. To be honest, I had never ventured past the wharf in Port of Spain or further than the Queens Park Savannah to the north of the city. I didn't know the city very well, but for the sake of encountering a Largahoo, I was prepared to familiarise myself with city night life. Like any city, it had its dangers once the blanket of night fell upon it.

One thing troubled me, however. There was this niggling fear that I could get lost in this big city. I heard too, the city had some real tough guys that roamed the streets at night, intent on robbing people. After all, this was the city and I was a country boy venturing into unchartered territory with nothing more than an inquisitive mind, a penknife, a couple cloves of garlic and a crucifix. My fears of the city's bad boys were far greater than those of the supernatural. Throwing caution to the wind I proceeded with my plan to explore Lapeyrouse cemetery in my search for a Largahoo in town.

I couldn't be certain where I first heard it, but someone had said they saw a Largahoo near Observatory Street, by the bridge, near the cinema on their way home. That area near Observatory Street really unnerved me whenever I passed there, whether it was daytime or night. Somewhere in the vicinity used to be home to slaves who toiled in the nearby sugar plantations. The entire Queens Park Savannah lands and surrounding areas were once sugarcane plantation. Maybe some of the ghosts from the dead slaves had returned to haunt the families of former slave owners! Whenever I think of that area near Observatory Street, the line from one of David Rudder calypsos always spring to mind; '*Out of them barrack yards calypso rising...*' I often wondered too, was this the area that CLR James chose to craft his novel *Minty Alley*? There was also a story of the famed calypsonian, Lord Kitchener migrating from Arima. On reaching Port of Spain, he was taken to a similar commune that housed other calypsonians in the city. I often wondered if it was the settlement near Observatory Street. That thought was never resolved.

One night, without any forward planning, I caught the last bus from Arima to Port of Spain. I must have fallen asleep at some point during the journey. When the bus finally reached the city, someone had to wake me. I was fascinated with all the ships and boats on the waterfront. The bigger ships just stood there motionless; the smaller crafts did a little synchronous dance on the surface of the water with the movement of the ocean. The city had a strange stench at night, far different to how I remembered Port of Spain in the daytime. Having wandered off in a totally different direction, I was none the wiser of how to get to Woodbrook, let alone Lapeyrouse cemetery. Despite all my careful planning in my previous expeditions, my failure to conduct any reconnaissance for this mission was beginning to show. Somehow, with some difficulty, I managed to negotiate my way back to Independence Square. From here, I had a much better bearing of my sense of direction in the city.

The city, while there were less people about than the daytime, was very much alive. It did surprise me to find there was so many people mingling about in the city at that time of night. Independence Square was buzzing with coconut and oyster vendors, their kerosene flambeau flickering in the light wind. There was a little van selling hotdog, and my mouth watered for one. Stray dogs were scavenging the bins, scattering rubbish on the roadside contributing to the stench of the city.

As I walked past a building; from upstairs, there was loud music and a raucous chorus of voices filtering out to the street below. Downstairs in the doorway, I saw a woman standing casually, smoking a cigarette. She smoked with the refined elegance and authority of a Hollywood movie star. I stood there for a few seconds admiring her exhale smoke into the foul city air. The woman wore a short denim skirt with a black lace-type blouse. The blouse was knotted at the front exposing her belly button on a flat tummy. She wore a pair of gold sandals, like those you saw masquerade revellers wearing on a carnival parade. Her deep red lipstick made her look hideous and out of character. She reminded me of a woman in our neighbourhood. Whenever my mother saw her dressed up in all her fandangle attire, she would always utter under her breath, "Look at the little jamette". It gave you the perspective that women who dressed like that were prostitutes. I contemplated asking her how to get to Woodbrook. I had second thoughts looking at her. I could not open my mouth to speak words, fearing she would start to cuss me. I learnt, sometime later, from a friend that the premises were a popular city nightclub. Calypsonians, as well as criminals and city businessmen, as well as prostitutes frequent the club. The club was a magnate for a lot of women who came there to make a good living from the affluent clientele. Taking another look at the woman, trying to avert my eyes from her plump cleavage, I went on my way.

I continued walking along to St Vincent Street, where there was a man laying a carpet of cardboard boxes in the doorway of a jewellery store. Bravely, I asked him how to get the Lapeyrouse cemetery. He looked at me with curious eyes and in a soft, well-mannered voice, "You looking for the dead?" He gestured with a cardboard box in one hand and motioned me to continue walking up St Vincent Street. Indicating with his hand to turn left at the next junction. He was very methodological in the way he gave directions, indicating what building you will see on the approach to the junction. The way he spoke reminded me of the principal at my first primary school. I watched him making his bed, wondering what had happened to his home. I braved another question, asking him what happened to his home. He looked at me, shook his head and said. "Never gamble". The city had many homeless people, in almost every shop doorway there was someone curled up sleeping on card or newspapers, some just on the bare concrete. Some slept on the park benches, covering themselves with layers of cardboard or, others open to the elements

Having followed the directions given, it dawned on me that I knew the area that led to Lapeyrouse cemetery. At a casual pace, it wasn't long before I reached the cemetery. This graveyard was fenced by a low stone wall, with a concrete archway at the entrance. The wall seemed to stretch endlessly into the night. I had learnt from the little time I spent at school that Dr Johann Siegert, the man who invented Angostura Bitters, is buried there in his family mausoleum. Also buried there are the famous artist Michel-Jean Cazabon, William Hardin Burnley – one of Trinidad's biggest slave owners, as well as slaves and other well-known Trinidadians. My mother used to say that at one time the man who managed the cemetery buried the common dead among the high-class ones, causing a lot of confusion with the authorities. The cemetery took its name from the French nobleman Picot de la Peyrouse, who is credited with being the first sugar plantation owner on the island. Today, the area is still dotted with remnants of French architecture, but most of the old houses have given way to modernisation. Some of the houses that survived are in dire need of restoration, others in dilapidation eroding a bittersweet memory of slavery and aristocracy.

Climbing over the low wall, I landed on a tomb. The tomb felt very fragile, and I thought it was about to collapse with my weight. Somehow, I found myself apologising to the grave, as if I had disturbed the dead who was sleeping there.

I laughed to myself, walking gingerly along the paved path in the desolate graveyard. I had been in a cemetery alone in the dead of night before, but nothing like this one. There were tall obelisks, Victorian tombs and ornate crypts that look like they belonged to French aristocrats. Some of these burial tombs were big enough for people alive to live in.

I remembered my mother saying that whenever you pass a cemetery, you should make the sign of the cross. I did so and tread carefully among the graves, stopping briefly to look at the intricate designs on some of the tombstones and crypts. It struck me how peaceful and quiet it was here. It was not at all frightening like many people think it is. I thought 'this is the ideal place for those seeking a little peace and quiet from the hustle and bustle of city life'. There was ample light filtering into the graveyard from the nearby streetlights, making it easy to manoeuvre among the graves. At times, I was certain that I saw something move in the shifting light. But there was nothing here, except the dead and me in this quietude.

As I strolled casually through the cemetery, I was suddenly aware that something was watching me, and there was a growling noise to accompany the stare. *Ah! Largahoo!* I thought. I felt for my garlic and crucifix. I put the crucifix around my neck and kept the cloves of garlic in my pocket. Stooping low, I searched in the dark for a loose rock for added defence. As I fiddled in the dark, I could hear two growling sounds coming from a nearby graveside. Instinctively, I search for another rock, proceeding with caution. My heart was pounding and my mind racing with the thought, *two Largahoos?* There was a little scuffle, I raised my hand with the rock, ready to toss it with an almighty velocity at whatever was in the darkness.

Nearing the spot where the growling was coming from, I saw two stray dogs squaring up each other over a huge bone. In the darkness, I couldn't tell if it was animal bone or human. At that point, I tossed one of the rocks at the dogs. They scampered away leaving the bone behind. I did not loiter to see if they would return to retrieve their bone. I roamed about the cemetery aimlessly, with an uneasy feeling. After about half an hour of waiting and peering at tombstones and crypts, I lost all hope of any Largahoo turning up. I scaled the low wall and took a different route back into Port-of-Spain. On reaching the bus terminus, I curled up on a bench and waited for the first bus back to Arima.

Some weeks later, approaching carnival season, I went to Queens Park Savannah for the Steelband Panorama competition. This presented the ideal opportunity for Largahoo hunting in Port-of-Spain once again. Having heard a couple of the bands play, it had gone past midnight, I decided to head towards Belmont Valley Road. This was one of the places where I had heard Largahoo existed, so I was more excited about this than the Steelband competition to be honest. I had no idea of the direction to Belmont Valley Road; my knowledge of Belmont was very vague. I must have wandered off and ended up on the Lady Young Road. On one side of the road were steep mountain ridges, the other, dangerous precipices leading into the valley below. For some reason, it felt that I should have been down in the valley. I could see the lights of the city below but all around me was total darkness. A lorry stacked with steelpans passed me heading east. I put my hand out to hitch a ride, but I suspected that the driver never saw me. Or maybe he did, and just ignored my pleading hand. Turning back and heading towards the city was not an option I considered. There was no way I was heading back towards the city, so I continued walking. I had no inclination of where the road would take me. However, I did recall, a time my cousins and I had walked from where they lived, and we had ended up on Lady Young Road. So, my instincts ushered me further on through the pitch-black night.

I was careful, choosing to walk in the middle of the road to avoid any reptiles lurking on the grassy verge. It made little difference, for it was so dark I could hardly see the road itself. If there was a snake in the road, I could have easily stepped on it and quite possibly have been bitten. The odd vehicle passed me heading in the opposite direction towards the city, but none going in the direction I was heading. After what seemed like hours of walking, streetlights appeared in the distance. I saw a Rotary Club sign informing motorists they were entering Morvant. I recognised where I was, feeling comfortable to be back in familiar territory and the welcome illumination of the surroundings.

Despite the trek, I failed to encounter any Largahoo or even a La Diablesse or, any living thing on my walk along this dark desolate road. My feet were sore, my muscles ached, and I was in dire need of a nice cool drink to quench my thirst. Not far ahead, as if my prayers were answered, I spotted a standpipe. Putting on a hasty pace, I arrived at the oasis. I cupped my hands for the cool water to collect in the reservoir of my hands, I drank until contented. After having my fill, I washed my face to refresh myself and ran the tap over my head. Feeling revived, I walked to the bus stop on the main road and waited for the early bus back to Arima.

After the carnival season had ended, I was relating to a friend in casual conversation about my escapade to Port of Spain in search of a Largahoo. He laughed until tears were streaming down his face. This guy was laughing in such a hilarious mockery of my misadventure that I wanted to hit him. He looked at me trying to put on a serious face, then burst out laughing again. "Boy you went in the wrong place to look for Largahoo. If yuh want to see Largahoo, go St James." I couldn't help but erupt into a laughing fit myself. I vowed, there and then, this was the last time I would venture anywhere in search of any Largahoo.

We laughed some more before he aimed a finger at an old tapia house in the distance. The iron roof was rusting away, the fence overgrown with wild vines. The coconut tree in the yard was abundant with green and dry coconuts. To the front, a tall moringa tree stood with good crop dangling from its branches like batons. The young mango tree to the front of the house was in full bloom. He looked up from the book he was reading, and with a straight face said, "Yuh know people say Bedesie is a Largahoo."

Papa Bois

Papa Bois

As a young boy, Papa Bois and Anansi were two of the first folklore stories that I was exposed to as a child. Anansi stories were full of humour, trickery, but more often, laughable sorrows. The Papa Bois stories were far from scary, serving more of a deterrent to those wanting to abuse the forest and its inhabitants. From my mother's tone in the stories, I think she was fond of Papa Bois, she had a kind of reverence for the Papa Bois's character. My mother was very sympathetic to wild animals and creatures. There were a few creatures she thoroughly disliked with a passion: snakes, cockroaches, mosquitoes, and crazy ants. These ants got everywhere; in the sugar, the condensed milk, food left on the stove, and even bread wrapped tightly in kitchen towels. These ants were a nuisance and left a horrible smell, I detested them more than my mother did.

Papa Bois, by and large, was there to protect the innocent animals from indiscriminate greedy hunters who hunted more than was necessary. I had heard numerous stories of hunters who became entangled in a web of vines as they stalked a deer, armadillo, or opossum in the forest at night.

These stories often came from hunters who returned empty handed from a long night of hunting with nothing to show for their perseverance throughout the night.

I am not certain if Papa Bois exists in all folklore across the Caribbean, but he is prevalent in St Lucia as well as Trinidad and Tobago. Papa Bois translates in French to mean 'Father Wood' or, as he is commonly known, as 'Father of the Forest'. This mythical shapeshifter can take the form of many forest animals to deceive hunters, protecting the forest wildlife from danger and excessive hunting. Some hunters would hunt many animals and offer the meat for sale while others hunted for their personal use. Being protector of the forest and its inhabitants, you could understand why Papa Bois would be furious with hunters who hunted his flock in their recklessness and lack of respect for his domain.

Papa Bois have been described as having a humanlike head with horns and an upper torso of a goat with human hands and feet of cloven hooves. He is strong and muscular and known by different name in other cultures. He is known as 'Maître Bois' (Master of the woods) and 'Daddy Bouchon' (hairy man) or as some refer to him as 'Father of the Forest'. Legend has it that if you met Papa Bois, it pays to be polite. If he should pause to pass some time with you, be cautious and never look at his feet. In all honesty, given the description of this creature, I can't envisage any sensible thinking person would to stop and converse with Papa Bois?

During my lifetime, I have not known of anyone who has ever seen Papa Bois. However, I have heard of many stories from experienced hunters, who confessed to having been deceived by Papa Bois, but not seen him. These stories often come to life when hunters return from the forest after a futile night of hunting. Sightings of Papa Bois were always described as a figure blending in with the forest environment.

I remember my first ever hunting experience as a young boy. I was aiming at a dove ready to pull the trigger when my friend said, "Papa Bois watching yuh boy". I must have shifted my aim or blinked. I squeezed on the trigger, missing the dove completely. "Ah tell yuh Papa Bois watching yuh!", he screamed in my ear. I shoved the gun in his hand saying, "Next time you shoot". Search as we may, neither of us saw another dove that day. We returned home empty-handed, except for a bunch of Cocorite (*Attalea Maripa)*, a succulent little palm fruit, as a consolation for our efforts.

Papa Bois was the protector of the forest; he wasn't there to cause harm or injury to people. The forest was his domain and he wanted you to respect it and all its inhabitants. He existed mainly to protect the wildlife that dwelled there and made the forest their home. Many hunters would confess to being entangled in a web of vines while stalking their prey in the dark mysterious forests of Trinidad. Like most folklore tales, Papa Bois stems from the rich traditions of African/European and French amalgamation of cultures, known as creole. It is this cultural blending that gives the region its colourful landscape of folklores that have become indelible in our society. The culture of folklores is embraced by everyone in the region, regardless of class, creed and race or colour.

My first attempt to find Papa Bois happened when I was about ten years old. I had gone to this swampy bog to collect Black Conches, a freshwater delicacy in Trinidad. These mud

Conches were a real treat when curried, and my mother often served them up with dumplings or warm *sada* roti. Black Conches were plentiful in this part of the forest and people claimed that the area was meant to be haunted by Papa Bois. So, this was a two-for-the-price-of-one trip. The idea of coming back with a good catch of Black Conches and the chance of catching a glimpse of Papa Bois was a prospect well worth the effort.

One of the things I learnt through listening to folklore stories, was that Papa Bois was not like a Soucouyant, La Diablesse or Largahoo who only roamed at night, he was guardian of the forest; protector day and night, the sentinel of the forest who never sleeps. The chances of seeing and meeting Papa Bois seemed greater than meeting any other Jumbies. So, I was hopeful and bubbling with anticipation.

In my head I had mapped out my encounter with Papa Bois. I had formulated several questions I was going to bravely put to him. The only difficult bit was which question to ask first. The questions ranged from how old he was and how he manages to be in so many forests simultaneously. *After all, Papa Bois is a good man, protector of the forest. He wouldn't mind me asking these questions, would he?* I tried to inveigle my friend into accompanying me to the forest to search for Papa Bois. Not even the lure of the Black Conches could tempt him. He was afraid to miss school and be flogged by his dad. I had heard his dad flogging him once, it was a ferocious assault. I often wondered if parents in those days went to special classes on how to brutalise their children. I made a little promise to myself, if I collected lots of Black Conches, I would give him some.

Being left alone to venture in search of Papa Bois. I took along my trusted dog, armed with a slingshot that I expertly made. I selected some nice, rounded pebbles, not forgetting a well-honed cutlass. My many visits to the forest made me well tuned with it. I knew which vines to cut to get a cool drink to quench my thirst, what wild bush to rub on my skin to counteract any brush with nettles or if I was stung by a bee or wasp. There was a hunter's tale that if you got stung by a scorpion, you should kill the beast, roast it, and eat the creature which serves as an antidote to the poison. Lucky for me, I never had to try this remedy as I was never stung by a scorpion. However, I did have sips of white rum that contained whole scorpions, a centipede, and various herbs.

Hunters believe that this mixture protected them from the poison of these creatures soaking in the alcohol liquid. I visited to a house in the countryside with a friend one Christmas time. The owner had a coral snake and another small black snake in a bottle filled with '*babash*'; a local, illegal distilled homemade rum. He offered us all a cap full of the liquid. Being a bit sceptical, I refused at first but then followed the crew as they all had a cap full. *What the hell, you can only die once!* I thought. The liquid had a sickly fresh smell but tasted only of *babash*. I knocked back the liquid and returned the cap to its rightful place.

One thing I did notice about the forest, the deeper you went into the interior, the less likely you are to find creatures such as snakes, scorpions, and centipedes. These creatures seem to prefer the fringes of the forest, nearer to civilisation. What I did encounter was more aggressive flying insects, like wasps, mosquitoes, and some dreaded black ants whose bite could render you with a raging fever. These ants were like leaf cutter ants but bigger, and they made a clicking sound as they scurried about the forest floor. These things, however, never worried me in the slightest. My mission was to encounter Papa Bois; I was excited, all other living beasts in the forest did not matter currently.

The area I intended to visit was well known for its abundance with wildlife. Maybe this was the reason for the many reports of Papa Bois sightings at the location. It wasn't a myth; the area was abundant with wildlife. On many occasions, I had encountered agouti, opossums, porcupines and once, I was lucky to spot an armadillo. Armadillos are great escape artistes. If you were hunting them, you had to be super quick with a shot. They would burrow into holes, and only if you were determined to dig them out would you stand any chance of capturing them.

To reach my destination I had to pass a huge tree that we named 'dead man tree'. It was so christened because there were always lots of bones scattered under the tree. It wasn't a Samaan tree, but its branches hung low creating a massive umbrella formation with a canopy almost bowing to the ground. The tree produced a fruit that bats seem to love very much. Some of bats even hung from the branches during the daytime, which was haunting and even worse, because we associated bats with vampires.

I wasn't scared of passing 'dead man tree' but the tree, even with a group, gave you a creepy feeling, especially when you saw bats darting about the canopy. It was just my luck that day, as I was passing 'dead man tree' there were lots of bats flying about. The sky had gone from bright blue to dark grey within a few minutes. I wasn't prepared for rain, and I thought maybe Papa Bois didn't like rain either. Maybe he much preferred to snuggle up in one of his cosy sheltering hideouts, watching his animals frolic in the rain. My dog didn't like rain either, lodging a complaint as the first droplets began unsettling him. Quickly, I cut some palm branches, constructing a makeshift tent to shelter from the downpour, under the canopy of 'dead man tree'. The dog was pleased too, giving me a thankful lick for the shelter.

This dog had a quiet snarl, his tongue would jut out his mouth showing his ferocious teeth. When he did this, it always meant he was ready to attack someone or something. As I looked out of the shelter, I saw an agouti foraging in the rain. I selected a nice smooth pebble from my pocket, placing it into my catapult, ready I took aim at the agouti. The silly dog licked my faced at the very moment I was prepared to fire a shot. The agouti, alerted to danger, darted off into the thick undergrowth. Just then, I recalled my friend's words, 'Papa Bois watching yuh boy'. I decided there I would not hunt, but traverse deeper into the interior of the forest once the downpour had subsided. The rain was nonstop for almost an hour and a half, and soon the tent started to take on water. The dog complained some more, I had to hold him close to me to comfort him. I thought to myself, what a big baby, afraid of a little water.

My first outing in search of Papa Bois brought no result. The torrential rain made it impossible to access the area to collect Black Conches. I was certain too, that Papa Bois wouldn't show in this kind of weather. I decided that the next time I ventured in search of Papa Bois; the dog was staying at home. The weather not only kept Papa Bois away, but it had also flooded parts of the forest too. I was thoroughly disappointed while Papa Bois was probably tucked away in a nice cosy canopy, relaxing to music of the raindrops cascading off the verdant instruments of the forest.

My punishment for my adventure was severe. The punishment did not feature the dreaded leather belt. Instead, my mum made me kneel on a metal grater, stripped of my clothes, placing two rocks in my hands to hold above my head. I was made to do this while she did her washing so she could keep an eye on me. As harsh as the punishment she inflicted was, it did not deter me in the slightest. Not long afterwards, a woodcutter known to our family was relating how he had seen Papa Bois. He was hauling logs from deep in the forest, when he saw the figure sitting on a log watching him.

I did a lot of pleading with the woodcutter, and my mother to allow me to accompany him the next time he went logging. It was the school holidays, so my mother obliged. She thought it would do me good and keep me out of mischief with the other kids in the street. Most of the time we just played cricket in a little clearing. When the ball got lost in the thick bushes and we were left idle, we often went hunting or, we would steal robe from the rope factory. We stole so much rope sometimes that we used to install swings on trees all over the forest. On some occasions, we would use the rope for harvesting *Cocorite*; or we would tie the rope tightly across two tree trunks and practice tight rope walking, something we copied from a circus that was touring the country. My memory doesn't recall anyone ever completing a tight rope walk, we would always fall over midway.

Going to this dense forest was a new experience for me. It was the furthest I had ever gone into a forest. Civilisation seem a whole world away from where we had ventured. This was new territory, led by an expert of the forest. This man knew the forest like the back of his hand. He was medium build, with rugged hands and hardly any muscles. I expected woodcutters to have well tone muscles and rugged. This was a small guy, tidy, meticulous, and very acute.

We drove there in his Land Rover; an old army vehicle with a green Gerry can secured to a bracket at the rear. In the back of the vehicle were two chainsaws with the word *STIHL* printed on them, an axe, a cutlass in a brown leather sheath and some rope. Throughout the journey there we talked about farming, the lack of respect for the land and the environment we lived in. He spoke about tough times, about how difficult it was becoming to make a living from logging, especially when you lose logs to thieves. This statement threw me a bit, I was intrigued, who would steal logs and why would anyone want to steal logs? It all became clear later that day when he explained it to me.

Once the woodcutters had fell the desired trees, they were brought to the edge of the forest. From here, they were then transported by lorries to various sawmills in preparation for manufacturing timber. Log thieves thrived on this ready availability of logs. They would turn with lorries and help themselves to the logs. They would then sell the logs to unscrupulous sawmills in other districts where they fetched a good price for both thieves and the sawmill. The story reminded me of a neighbour of ours. He used to drive a logging lorry, hauling logs to sawmills in the eastern districts. He was legitimately loading logs onto his lorry when he was set upon by a group of men who accused him of being a log thief. Despite his pleading, they set upon this innocent man, beating him so badly, he was hospitalised for several weeks, suffering broken bones and other internal injuries. It is not known if anyone was ever brought to justice for the vicious attack this man suffered. For several months he was unable to drive his lorry, and when he did resume driving, he drove a ready-mix concrete truck.

Once we got to the forest, everything was unloaded from the back of the Land Rover. I was charged with carrying the axe and the cutlass which I strapped around my waist with an army type canvas belt. The forest floor was teeming with leaf cutter ants hurrying along with intricate designs of leaf parts on their backs. We must have walked for nearly an hour, or so it seemed, along a clear path through the verdant forest. You could tell it was a well-used path by motor vehicles. I assumed it was tractors and lorries hauling logs. Suddenly, we veered into the belly of the jungle. The sound of the forest changed dramatically. The forest floor was damp, and I was glad that he loaned me a pair of rubber boots instead of the canvas shoes I had worn. In some places the forest floor had a lush green moss, so soft it was like walking on luxurious carpet.

All the while we walked along the clear path, his voice was at normal pitch when he spoke. Now that we were into the dense woods, his voice became a whisper. I thought to myself he probably didn't want to disturb Papa Bois. I was tempted to ask but reconsidered my thoughts, not wanting to offend his knowledge of the forest. Instead, I just observed this forest expert traverse through this emerald maze. As we walked along, he paused, stooping low, indicating with an outstretched arm and a soft whisper, "That is where I saw Papa Bois, sitting on that log." I followed his hand and found the log he was referring to. It was a huge log covered in thick green moss, almost blending in with the environment. An eerie feeling came over me as we continued deep into the forest. Having seen the assumed spot where Papa Bois was seen, my enthusiasm was heightened.

We had walked for a short distance; he stopped and marked a tree using his axe with a few notches. I thought, maybe it was a woodcutter's code. The tree had a daub of red paint and as we travelled further, I noticed other trees daubed in different colour paint, such as white, green, and yellow. This practice followed for several trees as we journeyed further into the forest. I assumed that it was only the trees marked with red paint were the ones he would be cutting. There were so many questions I wanted to throw at him but refrained from asking as I didn't want to come across as being annoying.

I was beginning to become anxious, having not had a single glimpse of Papa Bois so far. The woodcutter must have sensed my impatience. He motioned to a log, indicating we stop for some lunch. We sat on the damp log in a clearing, ate roti filled with fried *bodi* beans and drank coffee sweetened with condensed milk. As a treat, I was given a chocolate wafer biscuit. It was my favourite. I remembered them being advertised as the biscuit of Tarzan. Luckily for me that day, I was not going to do any swinging from vine to vine like Tarzan with a monkey on my back looking for Jane. Instead, I was conserving my energy for spotting the shape-shifting protector of the forest.

As we sat eating, he spoke softly, telling me of how woodcutters operate in the forest. The trees marked with red paint were selected for him to fall, other woodcutters used different colour paints. He explained that some woodcutters start from the first tree and work their way into the interior. He worked in the opposite, felling the last marked tree first, then working his way back. He explained that it made better sense to work this way. It meant when you were finished, you were nearer the edge of the forest rather than further into the interior. I threw a question at him. "Why notch the tree if it's already marked with paint?" He had a little grin and explained. "It is just to let other woodcutters know that you are in the area." I thought this was a very clever code used by woodcutters.

The woodcutter put his finger across his lips signalling me to be quiet. In the distance he pointed out a young fawn feeding on fallen fruits from a tall tree. "Some hunters shoot these small animals and dat angers Papa Bois." He whispered. As we watched the fawn, a huge *Mapepire zanana* (*Lachesis mut muta*) slithered past us, without the slightest of hindrance. I watched with awe as the snake disappeared into the undergrowth in deadly silence. By the time I lost sight of the snake, the fawn had also vanished. Maybe the fawn had caught scent of the imminent danger and manoeuvred to safer ground. Or maybe Papa Bois had alerted the little creature of the peril.

The woodcutter said many people had reported seeing Papa Bois in the vicinity where we were. This news raised my spirits, I began to feel hopeful again about seeing Papa Bois. With any luck, today would bring a chance to catch a glimpse of this mysterious shape shifting protector of the forest. I asked the woodcutter, "Has anyone ever spoken to Papa Bois?".

He looked at me with a curious disposition. "Boy I never know anyone who come close enough to speak to Papa Bois. I sure don't want to be the one to speak to him. You always see Papa Bois from a distance".

The woodcutter felled about ten huge trees that day. It was a thrill to watch him work and prepare the logs to be hauled from the depths of the forest. I played a small part trimming off the small branches with the sharp cutlass. He knew exactly how to cut the huge trees, so they didn't crash down destroying other smaller trees. He surveyed the area where the tree would fall, and they did, exactly as he predicted. Some of the trees produced at least three logs while others yielded just one. The woodcutter explained that is some areas you could use small tractors to haul the logs to the clearing for transportation to the sawmills. In areas inaccessible by tractors, oxen were needed to retrieve the logs. The logs he had prepared that day would have to be hauled using a strong ox, or sometimes two which he rented from a farmer who specialised in hauling logs. He was very much in favour of using the strong ox for hauling logs, rather than the tractors. He explained that they were more organic and better preserving the forest, plus the ox never got stuck in the soft areas like the tractors do.

It was late evening; across the forest you could hear a cascading call of cicadas and various other birds who took delight in chorusing high above the canopy of the forest trees. In the distance I could hear a woodpecker, or maybe two, creating a tremendous drumming on a tree trunk that echoed through the forest. "I think it might rain", the woodcutter said in a soft voice. He held the smaller chainsaw with an outstretched arm, indicating to another spot where he thought Papa Bois was sitting keeping an eye on him. I bravely asked him, "Are you not afraid of Papa Bois?"

He placed the chainsaw on his shoulder and replied. "If you not doing anything wrong, Papa Bois not going to bodder you. If you are destroying the forest indiscriminately, he does get damn vex. Dat is when yuh have to fraid Papa Bois."

I looked at him with some curiosity. Here was a man quite meticulous and caring for the environment that provided him a living. He showed great respect and abhorred others who treated it with disdain. It made me wonder, why couldn't we all be like this man? If we all showed a little respect for our surroundings, the world we live in would certainly be a much better place to live, enjoy and exist in harmony with each other as well as nature.

This man knew a lot about the forest. His knowledge did not only pertain to the forest but to the laws governing it as well. I was not aware, up until then, you required a permit to cut trees or remove any thing from the forest. Trees felled in the forest had to be recorded. I learnt that permits to cut and remove timber as well as other plants could be obtained from the local Warden Office. I was shocked to learn that some parts of the forest were privately owned and not the property of the state, as I previously assumed. I recalled an incident where someone had harvested hundreds of hardwood logs from a privately-owned forest. When the theft was eventually discovered there was not much evidence to go on that could substantiate any prosecution.

The woodcutter also enlightened me to the fact that, the law of the land is an ass. He pointed out that many of the birds that people kept in cages were in fact, against the law. I learnt too, that hunting between the hours of 7.30pm to 5am and using artificial lighting for hunting (Conservation Wildlife Act (CWA)); Chap 67:01 Sect 7(1) was against the law. People hunted extensively during these hours, and with artificial light. Clipping of birds' feathers to keep them captive was also prohibited (CWA Sect. 9 (1)), again, this practice was used for the domesticating of wild birds such as parrots, parakeets, and macaws. I couldn't understand why these things were allowed if it was unlawful. Maybe he did have a point after all. The law was, indeed, an ass.

The wealth of knowledge that this man imparted had me in awe. Birds such as Picoplat and Chicki-Chong were not permitted to caught and be kept in cages (CWA Sect; 4A (1) Part III), yet people did, in some cases quite openly. The conflicting thing is, although this was prohibited, the Act detailed dimensions of cages that these birds can be kept captive in, legally. Many of the snakes in Trinidad and Tobago were also protected under the Conservation of Wildlife Act 1958. The Act was subsequently revised and amended during 1963, 1980 and 2016 as the changing trends of society morphed with the times. I was very utterly surprised when I learnt that snakes were protected by law.

Most people in Trinidad and Tobago suffer from ophidiophobia, the fear of snakes, as I did for a short period in my early life. The general reaction to anyone encountering a snake was to kill it. I learnt from a television documentary that snakes were important to the ecosystem. Since watching the programme, I never intentionally harmed another snake.

We arrived back to the clearing where the Land Rover was parked. Today, there was no sightings of Papa Bois. The woodcutter however, never failed to identify the areas in the forest where he, as well as other woodcutters had supposedly laid eyes on Papa Bois. While I didn't disbelieve these reported sightings of Papa Bois, I couldn't be satisfied until I saw him myself. Fulfilling my own experience of a sighting remained the only real possibility, to attach certainty that Papa Bois roamed the forest protecting his flock of inhabitants.

While I was disappointed that we didn't see Papa Bois, I was satisfied with the experience I had that day. The experience and education of the forest had helped me to understand more about an environment where I thought my knowledge was extensive. As it turned out, I had known very little about the forest and its environment until then. I decided, whenever I next ventured into the forest, it was my intention to treat it with a bit more respect than I did, previously. My education of the forest was truly rewarding. Not just about the nature of the forest, but about the way logs are harvested and the effort involved in getting these logs to the sawmill to turned into timber. I was thrilled to learn of legislation in place to protect the forest, if only we could abide by it.

Unlike all the other ventures, my determination and expectation were high with the hopes of finding Papa Bois at some point in time. All the stories and leads that I had picked up were positive, as it was promising. But despite my optimism and my travels to the forests of Aripo, Cumaca, Valencia, Biche, Cumuto, Toco, Blanchisseuse and high into the Lopinot hills, I failed to get a glimpse of the elusive, shape-shifting Papa Bois. This setback didn't deter me in the least – if anything, it spurred me further. For some reason, I had this positive notion that I would eventually meet Papa Bois. The strangest thing was, whenever and wherever I searched for Papa Bois, there was always this eerie feeling that I was being watched.

In the still of the forest one day, for no apparent reason, I shouted at the top of my voice, "Papa Bois come out man, what yuh frighten for?". After the echo of my voice had simmered, the stillness of the forest was frightening. Not even the tress moved, the breeze ceased, it was as though every living thing in the forest stood spellbound, shocked at my outburst. It felt like everything had eyes and was watching me from every direction. I ran through vines and thick bushes until I came to a clearing. In the distance, I could hear motor traffic. When I emerged from the forest, it was a shock to where I had arrived. It was at the edge of a busy highway that connected the east of the country to the city. This had me puzzled; I was nowhere near to where I entered the forest. I found myself miles from the direction where I started. For weeks I grappled with the idea that Papa Bois may have disoriented me in the forest. I found no explanation for it, but I was not giving Papa Bois credit for it.

Papa Bois truly is the spirit of the forest, while I had never set eyes on him, a presence in the forest had startled me. Some months later I went into the forest in search of a bunch of *Cocorite*, from deep into the interior. I spotted an agouti in a clearing. Somehow, I had forgotten my pledge not to hunt again. With stealth action, I crept close as I could possibly get. I loaded a nice, rounded river pebble into my slingshot. Drawing the rubber strands with as much tension that I could possibly muster, I took aim. Above me I heard a rustling, as I looked up, I saw a huge Marabunta nest hurtling through the branches. I made quick ground to get away as it crashed to the ground, not far from where I stood. The nest shattered into pieces spewing swarms of wasps everywhere in frenzied anger. I eased away quietly, thinking *Papa Bois really looking after the animals for true.*

My interest in Papa Bois waned. No longer did I venture to the forest with the intent of finding Papa Bois. For some odd reason the sensation of eyes watching me and my encounter with the Marabunta's nest became the last conscious effort to find Papa Bois. I didn't make a concerted decision to relinquish looking for Papa Bois, but I made a conscious effort to stop hunting. I kept to fishing, conch collecting and crab catching. Maybe Papa Bois thought it was okay with these creatures as they were plentiful and provided a good food source. Once I had stopped hunting, I drew on a memory of my mother. She had never objected, but whenever I brought home birds from a hunt, she would always shake her head reluctantly when having to cook them for me. Although she never said it, I realised now, she was not in favour of hunting animals. Maybe Papa Bois himself was trying to show me there was alternative ways of hunting and gathering. I did have a paradigm, this deliberate decision changed my attitudes towards the forest, and the creatures that made it their home.

Some eerie events have transpired during my relentless search for Papa Bois in various forests of Trinidad. While I was disappointed having never come face-to-face to have a conversation or to even contemplate looking at Papa Bois's feet, I had grown to have great respect for the forest and its inhabitants. My adoration for the forest had sparked an interest in becoming a Forest Ranger. For many years it was all I envisaged as a career, I couldn't wait to come of age. However, as I grew to the age where I could have pursued a career as a Forest Ranger, my interest had dissipated. Two things were responsible for this curtailed ambition. I discovered girls; and that you needed about fifty O Levels and a driver's licence, neither of which I possessed due to a lack of formal education. This did not distract me from the fact that we should have a greater care, understanding, and the desire to treat our environment with the respect it deserved. Most people didn't really care much for the environment then. It was not a culture that was inherent in us at the time. We continued to pollute rivers and waterways, which resulted in heavy flooding, but never learnt from it. Today things are a little different, waterways are frequently maintained and there is a greater emphasis on education regarding our forest and the environment. Vulnerable riverbanks have been reinforced to prevent erosion. In some cases, the good that is done in one area has been counteracted by an undoing in another. Hillsides are constantly being pillaged of the vegetation that holds the soil together, cancelling out the efforts made to stem flooding in low lying areas. I believe there's a lot to learn about due care and diligence of our environment for long term sustainability. As folklore has it, Papa Bois is still out there in the forest protecting its animals, fauna, and flora from its greatest predator: mankind.

Once the idea of girls started to hold my interest, I soon forgot all about Papa Bois, leaving him to do what he did best: protecting the forest. Becoming a Forest Ranger was confined to the backroads of my memory and remained there, forever. I concluded that if Papa Bois should continue to protect the forest, he would need a lot of assistance from us humans. For no matter how elusive and mighty he may be, he is no match for man's obstinate disregard for the environment and his revolution for industry, commerce, and greed. I realised too, Papa Bois was teaching us environmental sustainability, long before the phrase became popular in modern lexicon.

Soucouyant

Soucouyant

Most of the folklores that exists in the Caribbean are born out of African traditions. The Soucouyant is by no means any different. The origins of the Soucouyant appears to have originated in the culture with the Soninke people of Senegal and some regions of Mali. The Soucouyant also exists in Ghana folklore too, with similarities to the Adze and can also be traced even to faraway places such as Mauritius. However, there are a few folklores that are very much East Indian in origin. Sadly, not many of these are commonly interrelated in the folklore settings of Trinidad and Tobago. One story that I remembered my own mother talking about, but never heard anywhere else, was the *churaille*. It is believed that the *churaille* was the spirit of a dead pregnant woman who had died in childbirth along with the unborn child. East Indian folklore has it that the *churaille* could be seen in the dead of night, wailing sorrowfully with her unborn child. The other tale I remember vividly was *Pitra paksh,* commonly referred to as *pitar pak*. Both my mother and my aunt, when I lived in San Juan had warned, during the *Pitra paksh*, you must be indoors before dark.

During *Pitra paksh*, it is alleged that the spirits of East Indian ancestors roamed the earth. These spirits according to folklore were not dangerous nor meant any harm. They were simply looking for closure for their souls. It didn't mean that some of them were not mischievous and devious. In Arima where I lived, no one really paid much attention to *Pitra paksh*. Although there was a large Indian community on the other side from our village, I seldom ventured there unless to play cricket.

When I arrived in San Juan to live, I had to adapt to a new lifestyle. My relatives there were practicing Hindus. Although my mother was a Hindu by birth, she observed Islam while my stepfather was alive as he was a Muslim by faith. My aunt was very particular in observing the *Pitra paksh* curfew. Having never subscribed to these supernatural tales, soon I was in all sorts of trouble for leading my cousins astray. My aunt even commented on the fact I was probably possessed by some evil spirit. She was not the only one to make that observation. Another thing that I had to adapt to when I lived in San Juan was the fact there were no paper in the latrine. Instead, I was shocked to find several rum bottles filled with water in neat row in the latrine. I never got used to that practice and would often liberate the classified section from the newspaper to assist me in that department.

The Soucouyant is well known across the Caribbean as a blood sucking fireball. She can be found in Haiti, St Lucia, Barbados, St Vincent, Guadeloupe, Jamaica, Dominica, Guyana, Suriname, and Trinidad and Tobago. In most of the Caribbean islands she is known as Soucouyant. In some

Caribbean regions such as Suriname she is referred to as Asema. Some call her soucriante or sometimes Lougarou.

A Soucouyant it is believed is an old woman who transforms herself into a fireball and flies off to prey on unsuspecting women in the night as they slept. Some say you can see the face of the Soucouyant at the centre of the fireball as she hurtles across the sky. Soucouyant victims are often left inflicted with sore blue/black marks on the soft tissues of their inner thighs, necks, or upper arms, sometimes on the hips or near the breasts, chiefly on women. She roams by night flying from village to town preying on her victims.

It has been said that the only way to capture a Soucouyant is to scatter rice in her yard before she returns. According to folklore, she must pick up every grain of rice before she can transform back into her human form. Should she fail to complete this task before sunrise, she would never be able to return to her normal skin. Salt could then be thrown to destroy her as she is left in agony, failing to transform back into her human skin.

As a boy, any old haggard looking woman would be deemed a Soucouyant, and there were many in our neighbourhood that fit the criteria. There was this old African woman who lived in a wooden house set back from the road. The property had no gate but was fenced off by some tall trees with dense foliage. The house was only visible from the gate entrance. The entrance itself was not gated.

I had never seen her husband, but she had four children, three boys and a girl. We both attended the same primary school, although we were not in the same class. She was a bit older than me, and you could say we were friends. At times, my school friends used to tease me and say she was my girlfriend. People said her mother was a Soucouyant and to this end, she was always teased and picked on at school. This girl was a fighter and would beat up anyone who spoke ill of her mother. Many times, she had come to my rescue when I was bullied at school. She would often invite me to her home where we roasted corn on the cob, which she harvested from their back-yard garden, or we would have Maggi chicken noodle soup in enamel cups. We sat on the back steps watching their chickens scratching and pecking at the dry earth.

I never asked or brought up the subject of her mother being a Soucouyant as I had this inclination that she wasn't. She was most certainly a Shouter Baptist, judging from the small shrine in the corner of the yard. One day, I tried to touch some of the articles near the shrine. This girl went berserk, she started to cuss me badly, in a derogatory way. That episode ended our friendship abruptly. It disappointed me that we were no longer friends. I missed the roasted corn and the chicken noodle soup and marvelling at the chickens scratching the earth. It was a sad way to end a friendship, but I was prepared to leave it at that. This meant that my concentrated efforts to find a Soucouyant now had to be focused elsewhere, since I had ruled out her mother as being one.

In a village called Carapo, on the outskirts of Arima, there had been many reported sightings of Soucouyant. People reported huge fireballs in the sky near the crossroads that formed a major junction heading to Carapo, Arima, Port of Spain and further east towards Sangre Grande. Every time these fireballs were seen, sure as there was day, you would hear of women that were victims of the flying fireball. It must have been a hot spot for Soucouyant or, maybe it was the same Soucouyant taking flight after she had assaulted her victims. I started to ask myself questions. Once the fireball landed, did she have to cool down before sucking her victim? And when she was through with her victim, was there some magic word to ignite her again to take flight and head off to the other prey? I had no answers.

Carapo was like a mecca for Jumbies. People were always reporting how they saw Largahoo, Douen, La Diablesse and Soucouyant in the vicinity. As a boy, I remembered hearing stories that were related by the only two taxi drivers that serviced the Arima to Carapo route. In those days there were not many cars on the road at night, and particularly taxis. These two drivers would relate to market vendors and passengers how many Largahoo they saw while working late at night.

One man recalled how he was lured into the depths of the forest near to a precipice by a La Diablesse. It was highly contested that he was drunk and got lost in the forest on his way home after a lengthy drinking session in the rum shop. His story did not collaborate with the landscape of the area. The terrain here was mainly flat land so, the chances of falling off a precipice was very remote. Despite the doubts about his story, other people claimed they had seen Largahoo on their way home after their late shift at the nearby industrial estate.

Apart from the reported sightings of Largahoo, La Diablesse, and Soucouyant; the junction was known to be haunted. The junction was a collision magnet. Many fatal accidents had occurred there and gave rise to stories that those who had lost their lives, returned to haunt the crossroads. The common talk was the spirits of the dead returned, looking to be reunited with their bodies. Taxi drivers and late-night workers in the nearby factories often gave accounts of either seeing or hearing evil spirits near the intersection. There was no shortage of Jumbie sightings in Carapo. Once it got past a certain hour of the night, very few people ventured walking the streets alone. Sightings of Soucouyant hurtling across the dark sky seemed to be a common thing in the surrounding villages near Carapo.

In the industrial estate, not far from the junction, there was a factory that made giant concrete cylinders used for underground drainage, bridges, and sewer systems. These concrete cylinders were so huge they could easily fit an adult inside with plenty of headroom. The factory would often store some of its stock on the grassy verge outside the compound. This made a good vantage post for me to position myself to stakeout any supernatural events during the night. The site wasn't far from the crossroads either which made a perfect lookout station. The cylinders would also provide good cover from the elements as I kept watch for any Soucouyant talking flight.

This was my first memory of a deliberate search for a Soucouyant. Like all my other haunts, I was full of excitement. *Tonight, would be the night something will reveal itself,* I hoped. I was always optimistic and full of hope when I ventured looking for these Jumbies. I spent most of the night trying to get comfortable inside the concrete cylinder. If trying to get comfortable wasn't challenging enough, I fought a constant battle with mosquitoes throughout the night. All I managed to achieve for my efforts that night was around a thousand mosquito bites and glimpse of early morning workers as the nearby highway roared with the sound of lorries and construction traffic.

Daylight began to make a grand appearance. The eastern sky became a canvas of shifting hues of various shades of gold, orange, reddish bronze, yellows, and a mist of pink. The highway was alive as the sun climbed higher into the sky washing the canvas with a powder blue. I gathered myself - cold, disappointed, and tired, I made my way home on foot.

Over the next few weeks, several women in my neighbourhood were comparing bruises on various parts of their bodies where they had been sucked by Soucouyant. My own mother did not escape the bloodsucking fireball. I saw the Indian lady next door lifting her dress at the fence to show my mother the Soucouyant wound near her crotch. All sorts of ideas began to race through my head. I was thinking if all these women being attacked, the Soucouyant must live nearby. No one, apart from my friend's mother, came anywhere close to fitting the Soucouyant profile. Somehow, I still did not believe she was a Soucouyant. I was petrified to venture near her house to investigate, fearing her daughter would see me and beat the life out of me. I wasn't afraid of her, but I knew I was no match for her fighting skills. This was one girl you did not want to mess with.

On the other side of the village from where we lived, there was an old woman who lived on her own. Her garden was overgrown with shrubs and some beautiful peach rose bushes, with a heavenly scent. I began making notes about her in my school copy book. It became habitual for me to walk the long way home just to make detailed observations of this woman and her house. It wasn't a huge house and – apart from the overgrown garden – the yard was always clean and the paint on her house was always vibrant.

One day, I spotted her in the yard making a cluck, cluck noise with her mouth as if she was beckoning chickens. People made this noise when they were summoning their chickens at feeding times. She appeared to be scattering some sort of grains on the ground. I stood there watching her and making notes, no chickens came. I moved closer to the gate peering in, she must have had eyes behind her head. She spun around shouting, "Get your magga ass from my front gate, yuh little wretch!" I ran away as fast as I could, not wanting to see her face. It was rumoured that she only had half a face. I couldn't say for certain how true it was. She did, however, have a cloth wrapped around from her head, covering the sides of her face. It was said that a jealous lover had thrown acid on her, when she was much younger, disfiguring her face.

This old woman made a good candidate for a Soucouyant. I began to question my mother about the woman. Bravely, I asked my mother if she believed the woman could be a Soucouyant. My mother laughed, in a kind of cynical mocking way to my question. She normally did this when she found you were making an ass of yourself, or you were crossing a line you shouldn't. My mother looked at me questioning "Boy yuh have light up in yuh ass or what?"

I did not respond to her question, but she did take some relish in saying, "Dat woman cyar suck mango, let alone be ah Soucouyant." I took solace in the adage, 'mum knows best' and never asked another question about the potential Soucouyant.

I now faced a dilemma: where was I going to look with the hope of finding a Soucouyant? Luckily for me, there were a lot of Soucouyant stories floating around the neighbourhood. Yet nobody had a clue as to who, or where this Soucouyant came from. This Indian girl who lived on our road claimed to have been a victim of the notorious Soucouyant too. This girl was dark in complexion, compared to her other siblings. Her skin, almost like velvet to the touch. One day, I don't know why, but she showed me a spot on her thigh where Soucouyant had troubled her.

This girl was having a relationship with an African guy living opposite to them. Her parents, suspecting the relationship, were dead against the union. I had taken a liking to this girl as well, so to get a glimpse of intimate parts of her body was a delightful opportunity. This girl would call me over to show me where Soucouyant had sucked her. It included the inner parts of her thighs near her crotch, the sides of her breast or near her navel, and one time on the rump of her buttocks where Soucouyant had attacked her during the night. To be honest, I don't think I ever noticed the Soucouyant marks. I was more interested in the parts of her body that I was privileged to set eyes on.

I began to question myself. Why would a right thinking Soucouyant leave the exposed neck or arm to go under the clothing to suck her victims? And why is this flying fireball only sucking women? None of these answers were available to me, but it was an intriguing scenario. Maybe, if ever I were to encounter a Soucouyant, I would put my crucifix around my neck and boldly pose the question, "So, why you only sucking woman?" The thought was as absurd as it was ludicrous the moment it came to mind.

One night, returning from a late show at the cinema, something strange happened to me. I must add, at this point, back then there were no planes or helicopters flying about at night, especially not after midnight. I make this point because the airport was a couple miles from where we lived, in fact the flight path was over our house. As the saying goes in Trinidad, anyone up at that hour, are either Jumbie, haunted people, or men who like to *drevay*. I fell into the latter category.

As I walked home, along that long, dark, deserted road, I crossed a bridge that sent a weird shiver through my body. The hairs on back of my neck stood to attention. Dense forest populated both sides of the road. You could hear the Jumbie birds, crying out from the tall trees along the riverbank. The eeriness of this bridge was odd for several reasons. It wasn't just me that had this experience. Quite a few people had complained of similar chilling sensation that came over them when crossing the bridge, whether it was day or night. Nothing sinister had ever occurred at this bridge, or at least nothing that anyone had connected with the odd supernatural sensation experienced by people crossing the bridge. This bridge was creepy to everyone during daylight hours, so you can only imagine the shivers it sent through your body crossing it at night. There was the dense forest on both sides, the chatter of nocturnal creatures and the chilling shriek of the Jumbie birds to compound the eeriness.

Walking further, the road became punctuated with houses and the streetlights were closer together. This welcomed illumination did not last. Within a few hundred metres, the lighting extended further apart. The forest, however, was less imposing, just on one side of the road and a few houses on the other. At this hour, they were all in darkness as their occupants had long retired. Nearing the road that led to my house, above the forest, I saw this circular light hovering in the sky. Frozen to the spot, I rubbed my eyes vigorously looking up again. The light was still there hovering. Instantly, I wanted to pee, as well as run like hell. I stood in the middle of the road and had a pee, keeping a fixed gaze on this mysterious light. I stood there looking up at this light. I did not, for one moment think this was a Soucouyant. The light did not display the fireball characteristics associated with that of a Soucouyant. The sight of this light stunned me, and I was at a loss of what it could be.

The experience had me spellbound. As I stood there transfixed, I realised there was no more pee coming out. I looked behind me in earnest, hoping to see another human heading home to draw their attention to the phenomenon. The road was empty except for me, my shadow and a trail of urine snaking its way along the road. I kept my gaze on the hovering light. The light appeared to be watching me, watching it. The light certainly wasn't a fireball, akin to that of a Soucouyant, and this had me further intrigued. It looked more like a giant spotlight without a beam, and strangely, it wasn't staying put. I continued walking in the direction towards the mysterious light. There was a rustling in the bushes, turning to have a look, I saw nothing. When I returned my gaze, the light had disappeared. I became frantic, looking all around me and up at the sky wanting the light to return. There was nothing to be found. I stuck my hand in my pocket, wrapping my fingers around the penknife. In my head it wasn't clear what I would have done, but it was reassuring to know I had my trusted penknife. I lingered about for another ten minutes banking on hope the light would return. It never did. A couple of metres ahead of me, I saw a human figure casually walking, then disappearing into the darkness. I turned into our road and walked backwards until I reached my house, entering backwards as my mother had advised ever since the Largahoo episode.

Next day, I related the tale to my mother. She was unimpressed by my encounter, instead, she went on to scold me saying, "Jumbie up in yuh ass? You wouldn't be satisfied until some La Jabless pick up yuh ass and drop yuh in a ditch." This woman really had a way with words that never failed to amuse me. I dared not laugh as it would have infuriated her further. Inside, I had a quiet chuckle.

Throughout all my escapades, I had never once encountered a single Jumbie, in any form, fashion or disguise. What I can attest to, was the experiences had taken me to some strange places, with odd occurrences that will stay with me always. They didn't instil any new beliefs or doubts or discouraged me from my inquisitive escapades. What it did do was fuel my enthusiasm for adventure. A few days after I had seen the light in the sky, the Indian girl revealed to me again, Soucouyant sucked her twice in one night. This had me seriously puzzled. Did the Soucouyant suck her and returned, or was it two separate sucks in the one visit? There was bruising on her cleavage and on the inside of her thighs. She even let me touch the spot where she was bruised. Don't know why, but I asked her if it hurts. She smiled, shaking her head to mean no. I touched the spot again, my eyes fixed on her cleavage. She saw my gaze and kissed my lips. Somehow, the kiss did not register with my lips. Instead, it baffled me more than ever. There was so many questions and doubts swirling around in my head, I did not know what to think. How could you be sucked by this evil flying fireball, and it not hurt? Nevertheless, these supernatural folklores became more and more intriguing. I was still hopeful of encountering one of these Jumbies. The question, however, remained: when? I touched my lips where she had kissed me and went home totally confused, both by her kiss and the Soucouyant bruising.

I was well into my teenage years when an opportunity to witness a Soucouyant in flight came to me gift-wrapped. I was dating this girl from San Rafael, a country area in east Trinidad. She was much older than me and had a young child. My mother questioned my motives and relationship with this woman. She went on to ask me if I was looking for a stepfather job. Although this girl had never seen a Soucouyant herself, she claimed one had sucked her once. Her brothers and her mother, however, bore witness to seeing the flying fireball in the sky. Finally, I thought, here was my chance for an encounter with a Soucouyant. By this point I had invested in a cheap camera, so I reckoned there was a good chance of capturing an image of the blood sucking vampire.

San Rafael was real country area with dense forest. The only streetlights were on the main road at the junction and in some selected streets. Once you veered off into a country lane, you had to use flashlights to find your path, unless you knew that path like the back of your hands. The junction at San Rafael was thought to be a haunted place. A group of missionaries including the Governor Don Jose Leon de Echales were slaughtered there by the Tamanaque tribe in 1699. The tribe were eventually hunted down by the Spaniards. Some of the tribe committed suicide rather than be taken captive. Many of the captured tribe were executed and some enslaved. The bodies of the missionaries were recovered and their remains eventually laid to rest inside the church in tombs. It is believed that the ghosts of the missionaries roamed the junction by the church in the restless hours of the night.

This woman I was dating lived on a working cocoa estate, about three miles from San Rafael junction. After the three-mile journey, you had to walk a further half mile through lush acres of orange and cocoa plantation in total darkness before arriving the house. During the early hours of the evening, it wasn't difficult to get a taxi there. Anything after 10 pm at night, was a struggle to get a taxi there or back to Arima. I used to time my visits in such a way that it involves me spending the night there, much to the annoyance of her mother.

The entire family was now intrigued by my obsession to spot a Soucouyant. One of the brothers even told me he came face to face with a Largahoo on his way home one night. For some odd reason I did not believe him, neither did anyone else. My girlfriend's mother mentioned out of the blue that she had woken up in the middle of the night to go toilet, only to find a vampire bat sucking away at one of her younger son's toe. In all my life I had never seen a vampire bat but heard a lot about them. They would generally feed on animal's blood but were known to enter homes and feast on sleeping humans.

One of my girlfriend's brother took me to a cocoa house a short distance away from the main building. Here he showed me two vampire bats suspended from the rafters of the cocoa house. He said they were White-winged vampire bats (*Diaemus Youngi*). I must admit these bats were quite different from the common black bats that fly about in chaotic coordination at dusk. They were brownish in colour, cinnamon like, and had oddly shaped ears and white along the edges of their wings. As my guide shone the flashlight on them, they began to stir then darted off into the darkness. Quite possibly to have a little blood feast.

We had to walk about a mile from the house, through some dense bush before arriving at a clearing at the top of a small hill. From here, I was told you could see the Soucouyant flying across the sky. I was curious. "Did you ever see her face?", I asked.
"Nah too far away", the younger brother intervened. The older brother had armed himself with a shotgun, the others had machetes and high beam flashlights that cut through the darkness like samurai swords slicing watermelons. I could hear the rumble of a vehicle in the distance. Before I could

put forward the question, the younger brother volunteered the information, "Rangers heading up to the dam".

Someone shone a flashlight on a tree in the distance, "Aye look ah big manicou (*Didelphis Marupialis*) boy!". The guy with the shotgun took aim but did not shoot. Instead, pointing with the gun he said, "You see over dey, dat is where we saw the Soucouyant flying".

I was struggling to make any sense of it at all. For all I know, he could have been pointing at the moon. My head was confused, what would a Soucouyant be doing all the way out here in the middle of nowhere? There were no houses nearby with the prospect of potential victims. However, I was going on their hunch. They had seen a Soucouyant before, so I was prepared to be patient. I remembered a friend of mine used to say, "With patience you would see an ant's belly". If this was so, then one of two things could happen here: I would either see a Soucouyant in flight tonight or an ant's belly.

One hour passed, which turned into two, and so it continued. During this time mosquitoes were having a feast with my blood. Maybe they were allies with the Soucouyant and vampire bats, sent on reconnaissance to get some of my blood. After several hours and the approach of dawn, we all started to head back to the house. The younger brother said nonchalantly, "I feel dat Soucouyant woman gone back Grenada".

I thought to myself, they have an inclination of who transforms into the Soucouyant? That night, I saw neither an ant belly nor a Soucouyant for that matter. I just about hid my disappointment. The saving grace was, I could go back to the house into the warm embrace of my girlfriend.

Some abnormal activities were swirling around in my head when the word Grenada was mentioned. Why would a Soucouyant return to Grenada? All the women who were suspected of being a Soucouyant were either from St Vincent, Grenada, or Martinique. I had this absurd notion that maybe these Soucouyant flew over from the Islands to Trinidad, suck their victims, and flew back before dawn. Maybe that could be the reason why none had ever been caught. The idea was so farfetched, it was not worth giving it second thoughts. But then, maybe it wasn't. My mother had narrated a story many years ago of a Soucouyant from Port of Spain, possibly Charlotte Street. This Soucouyant flew to England to steal a golden spoon from the Queen. The story didn't say if she went to Windsor Castle or Buckingham Palace. On her return with the spoon, it fell into the sea near the Bocas. Legend has it that the glow from the golden spoon could still be seen in the ocean. So, the possibility exists that these Soucouyant could well be island hoppers. Flying over, having their fun and head back before dawn.

One of the things I began to examine as well, was the fact that women who had been victims of Soucouyant assault, always had these marks on intimate parts about their body. These blotches were often associated with prolonged kissing of the tender areas of the skin and could be displayed on both men and women and known as hickeys, generally seen on the neck: a Soucouyant trademark scar was identical to that of a hickey. This started to make a lot more sense to me. Now that I was older, and acquired a more mature understanding about intimacy, it became a lot more lucid. I came to conclude that these blotches that women discreetly displayed to each other were nothing more than marks of intimacy. There was no other reasonable or plausible explanation for the marks on these women. It dawned on me the use of subterfuge by the Indian girl. She had used me as a clever distraction while she pursued her relationship with her African lover. Seeing us together, people got the impression that something was going on between us. This steered the focus away from the other guy, such deviant distraction by this young woman, it was ingenious. The comfort from that was, I became privileged to parts of her body that I wouldn't have seen under normal circumstances.

Since my experience with the hovering light that night, I never saw or got near enough to any Soucouyant experience again. The Indian girl stopped showing me her bruises after she learnt I had a girlfriend. Her relationship with the African guy became public knowledge. They were eventually married, and ironically, moved to San Rafael to raise a family. I asked her if any Soucouyant had sucked her since. She smiled showing her brilliant white teeth, without an answer. I drew my own conclusions from her response and took that as a no. She put a kiss on her finger and placed it on my lips. My mother's words came to mind, 'you little Jamette.'

A few years later, I was watching a movie in the cinema with Arnold Schwarzenegger and Grace Jones. Schwarzenegger was making love to this woman who suddenly turned into a ball of fire, her face visible in the flames. She flew off into the night with bellow of cackling laughter. Someone in the audience shouted out. *'Soucouyant boy.'*

As the years went on, most of the forested areas where we lived was lost to housing and industrial developments. Sightings and attacks by Soucouyant dwindled away, slowly. Even in faraway country lanes where electricity had managed to penetrate, the chatter of Soucouyant and other Jumbies became few and far. Increased night life in towns brought extended taxi service, eliminating the need to walk and encounter any of these nocturnal Jumbies.

Throughout my search for these Jumbies across Trinidad, one thing that remained a mystery in my hometown, Arima. There was this house on the main road leading to Arima. There was speculation that the old the woman who lived there, was a Soucouyant. I walked past this house during schooldays and much of my adult life, never had I witnessed anyone entering or leaving the property. No one I knew had seen the woman who lived in the house, yet everyone knew it was a woman who lived there. Maybe she was indeed a Soucouyant who had flown back to Grenada, or worse, drowned trying to retrieve the golden spoon from the Bocas.

Having spent a great deal of time searching and exploring for Soucouyant and other Jumbies, I was no closer to having any success. I was struggling to find any shred of evidence that could substantiate, or at least give me a hint of, their existence. Despite this, Soucouyant stories did pop up every now and again. I did notice, especially with my mother and other women in the neighbourhood as more households acquired electricity, fewer people became victims of the Soucouyant. The female species in the neighbourhood no longer gathered by their fence to display signs that Soucouyant had sucked them.

One Saturday morning, the strangest thing happened to me. I was browsing through the open market in Arima, passing time before going to work. This old woman, dressed in a blue gown and head tied with a black cotton cloth, approached me. She looked at me from head to toe, in a measured, calculated, and uncanny stare. I swore she could have seen inside my body with the look she gave me. She waved her finger at me and said, "You going to meet yuh match one day". I had never seen this woman before and have never seen her since. The encounter troubled me that day, but it was soon forgotten.

La Diablesse

La Diablesse

To my recollection, only men had ever encountered La Diablesse. I had never come across, or heard of, any woman who was lured by a La Diablesse. Like most of these folklores, these creatures always seem to have some feature of an animal and the La Diablesse was no exception.

Folklore legend has it that the La Diablesse was once a beautiful woman. She had made a deal with the devil that went sour, and subsequently transformed her into the demon she is today. She is thought to have a hideous face but adorns herself in long flowing beautiful French frock and sweet-smelling perfume. She dons a wide brimmed hat to hide her hideous looks from inquisitive men. She has one human foot and one cloven hoof. To fool her unsuspecting victims, she would always walk on the edge of the road with her cloven hoof on the grass verge. Once a man is lured by her alluring charms, he is led into the forest where she leaves him confused and lost. It is said, many men had come to their demise by either falling over a precipice or into river.

There are many tales of men who have survived the traumas of an encounter with a La Diablesse. Often, men who encountered a La Diablesse were drunk and on their way home through dark country lanes. It was common for people to use shortcuts on dark moonless nights to find themselves home. I remember hearing the tale of a gentleman who had encountered a La Diablesse on his way home. He claimed that the devil woman had lured him into the dense bushes after seeing her standing on the roadside. She took his hand and was mesmerised by her sweet scent. When he came to a state of consciousness, he was knee deep in water in a fast-flowing river down a valley in the Northern Hills. Not a lot of people believed him as he was a known womaniser who would, on payday, drink himself into a drunken state before leaving with an opportunist female from the rum shop.

I heard that the women he went off with would always trick him. They would bamboozle him with sweet talk and sexual promises, then take his all his money, abandoning him, drunk on the roadside. Monday morning, he could be seen chasing down the loan sharks that circled around the banks and rum shops, preying on these desperate, broke, and unfortunate men. Who knows maybe these loans sharks were the modern day Largahoo? They often sported big gold chains around their necks and their enamelled teeth replaced with flashes of gold.

Sightings of La Diablesse was a regular thing on the undulating narrow road leading to the North Coast of Blanchisseuse. Once you crossed a section of that road there were no streetlights. It is no exaggeration when I say if you held out your hand in front of you at night, it was impossible to see it. Sometimes even if the moon was out, it still was very dark, with the lush canopy of trees keeping the glow of the moonlight away.

It has been said that the one sure way of scaring away any La Diablesse, or evil spirits, was to wear your clothing inside out, even your underwear. I was not prepared to follow this rule. After all, I didn't want to scare this evil belle, I wanted an encounter. My fear that night wasn't the encounter with a La Diablesse, but the thought of being picked up by police who regularly patrolled the area. And the only way to encounter a La Diablesse was to stay on the path of the road. It was from roadside verges that she lured these drunken opportunists to either death or serious injuries.

It would have proven to be quite a task explaining to police officers what I was doing on the road, at that hour of the night. It was a challenge I was not prepared for, so with the slightest sound of an engine, I camouflaged myself in the nearby bushes. There was no way I could possibly justify being so far away from home. I had to laugh at myself for thinking I could be honest and confess that I was looking for La Diablesse. Such a confession could have easily earned me a free ride in the back of the police jeep, and subsequently in a cell at Arima police station. So, rather than risk a free ride and a night accommodation, I proceeded with being precautious.

I had reached a path that matched the area where it was alleged that the La Diablesse had lured the drunk. The man had suffered some horrific injuries after falling over a precipice. Far down below a steep gorge, I could hear in the darkness the rushing current of the river below. The forest was alive with an orchestra of voices from its inhabitants.

Some sounds I recognised, the others I had no clear clue of what made those weird noises. At one point I wanted to believe it was monkeys but wasn't sure if monkeys roamed about at night. It could well have been Papa Bois himself with a code warning the other night dwellers that the Jumbie hunter was lurking.

In the distance I recognised the rumble of an engine. It was difficult to judge from which direction the vehicle was approaching. Crouching low down in the nearby bushes on the verge to keep hidden from view, I waited. The vehicle seemed to take forever on its approach making me impatient. The fear of some creature crawling over me was starting to make me uncomfortable. As the sound of the engine drew nearer, I could tell it was a police Jeep. They were travelling at a dangerous speed on this narrow road. The beams from headlamps had sliced the darkness like a laser beam. I was certain the officers had spotted me. The vehicle slowed to a crawl. A sense of relief came over me as the vehicle accelerated on the precarious bend, speeding off, heading towards Arima. As I came onto the road, two huge mountain crabs scurried across the road disappearing into the bushes without any haste or care that I was there. Only after they had vanished did the thought entered my head that I should've caught them.

Crabs running about meant that rain was on its way. I continued walking along in anticipation of meeting this demon belle of the night. After about half an hour walking, encountering many more crabs and a few snakes gliding across the tarmac, I decided it was not viable to venture any further. If I continued at this pace, I would be in

Blanchisseuse by morning. Retrieving my penknife from my pocket, I cut a few lengths of thin vines that hung loosely from trees overhanging the roadway. I waited for a few moments in the middle of the road with anticipation that something might happen. That hopefulness was short-lived, and I began walking in the direction to Arima.

In the distance I could hear what sounded like the ocean, soon huge raindrops started to attack me. There was a sudden flash of light that spilt the sky, followed by a crack of thunder. By now I was drenched, in the middle of the night, far away from home and shivering cold. All sorts of foul language left my mouth that night. Internally, I was vowing to kill any La Diablesse that dared to appear before me now. The thought was ludicrous.

The La Diablesse must have either heard me or, read my mind that night, for none appeared; even Largahoo was taking shelter from the rain. I had not gone far along the road before I noticed crabs scurrying along the road in all directions. I selected the bigger ones, placing my foot on their backs and tying their pincers with the vines I had gathered earlier. Within a short time, I had caught more crabs than I could carry. Soon, I was in more familiar territory with houses on both sides of the road. There were streetlights and it felt like civilisation had revealed itself again, having abandoned me for several hours.

My mother wasn't best pleased with me when I returned home at the break of dawn, drenched and shivering. Bless her soul, she made me some strong Hong Wing coffee. I dried myself, drank the coffee before retiring for some well-deserved rest. My mother was grateful for the crabs. She emptied them into a bucket, pouring hot water over them. That day we enjoyed some good, curried crab with coconut dumplings and boiled cassava. The La Diablesse hunt had had some rewards, but unfortunately, not the right one.

I couldn't help wondering why I was never encountering any of these mysterious Jumbies that seem to haunt people all over the island, but never seen by me? Maybe these Jumbies were afraid of me, or Papa Bois must be communicating with them, warning them off. Whatever it was, I certainly wasn't having a great deal of luck finding these demons of the night and those that roamed by day.

A few weeks after my escapade to find this La Diablesse, a friend related a story to me. He said that the road was really and truly haunted. A man had cut off his lover's head after he found out that she had another lover. People had often claimed to have seen a headless woman roaming the night in the vicinity of the ice factory, where it had happened. Years later, while working at the bar, I met the man who stumbled upon the head. He relived the night to me when he stumbled on the head. He himself was visiting a lover in the area. He recalled being half drunk and walking along when he kicked something, he thought was a ball. On inspecting it, to his horror found it to be the head of a woman. He dropped the head, closed his eyes, and ran all the way to Arima Police Station to report the incident. The irony of it is, the man who was allegedly responsible for beheading the woman, was my barber when I was younger. It baffled me why my mother, who knew this, would have sent me to have my hair cut by a convicted killer.

One day while he was cutting my hair, I asked him. 'You ever see any La Diablesse?' He paused, then continued snipping away at my hair, then said. 'Dis place, ha boy, it full ah Lajabless. If yuh ever see one, run like hell yes!' When he was finished cutting my hair, I handed him the money for the haircut. He looked at me and shook his head. 'Nah doh worry, dis one on the house.' I thanked him for the generosity and skipped along, feeling pleased. I never went back to him for another haircut. I often wondered what he meant by 'Dis place full ah Lajabless.' Did he encounter many La Diablesse in his time, or was he referring to the folklore traditions? Or was he talking about the women who lured vulnerable men drunken with lust? Maybe he himself had encountered a few La Diablesse in his time. Truth be known, I wasn't prepared to ask him another question ever.

My search for a La Diablesse came to a natural end, I think without me even realising it. As I got older, I lost a lot of interest in seeking out these demon belles of the night. I noticed a peculiar thing about the La Diablesse, she seemed to have derived from a French, middleclass creole background, from the way she dressed and the sweet scent of perfume that accompanied her presence. Maybe La Diablesse had modernised and acquired plastic surgery and was now walking about in high heels, miniskirts, and jeans. They may have moved with the times and out of the darkness where they now sought their victims in nightclubs, discos and parties luring more men now than ever. Only now they were no longer luring their men to death but giving them a death sentence.

Many years later, of all places, in London I met the spirit Diablesse. Browsing through a food store in Kensington I saw this bottle of rum staring me in the face. I could not believe it! After all these years and those dark nights searching for this demon belle, she was residing in England all the while. Well! I had to laugh. Is like La Diablesse say, "Aye man! Look meh." I was left with no choice but to grab the Diablesse and take her home with me. The spirit and I had enjoyed a mellow moment. She was warm, full of spice and her cinnamon complexion complimented her citrus aroma. My glass was finally empty and the spirit of the Diablesse was gone.

Mama Glo

Mama Glo

To be completely honest, I have not heard of many people who have come across Mami Wata or Mama Glo as she is known, especially in Trinidad and Dominica. The name Mama Glo derives from the French Maman de L'eau meaning 'mother of the river'. In Guyanese folklore, she is also known as Mama Wata.

According to Caribbean folklore, she has the upper body of a beautiful woman, the lower half of her body was mermaid like. She has a forked tongue and as the legend goes, she tends to her tresses with a golden comb. Mama Glo is noted to be the protector and healer of the aquatic animals. It has been said she is the companion of Papa Bois.

The legend of Mama Glo can be traced back to West and Central Africa and some parts of Southern Africa and was transported to the Americas through and during the African slave trade. Her legend is deeply rooted in the *Orisha* and *Oshun* goddess of African culture. Mama Glo, by all accounts, is a freshwater mermaid-like creature. I did wonder if she knew she had some saltwater cousins. And, if so, did she know they were related?

Throughout my childhood and into adulthood, I can recall only two instances where I heard about Mama Glo. The first instance being where she had lured a man to drown in Valencia River. The other was a place called Blue Basin near Diego Martin. It was said that Mama Glo held the man under the water, but he was saved when a group of people arrived at the Blue Basin for a swim. Both these places had large pools ideal for swimming. Valencia River has always been a bit treacherous, even for a good swimmer. I was a regular swimmer at Valencia River, but I had never ventured further than the popular bathing areas.

When I visited Valencia River on this occasion in my search for Mama Glo, I decided to venture further up the river to an unchartered area. Getting to where the man had drowned was precarious terrain. There was no clear path to this secluded pool and in some places, there were steep slopes leading down to the river. This was a ferocious river when it rained, especially if it rained high in the mountains, unknown to those bathing in the valley below. It brought great volumes of water gushing down from the mountains along with tons of gravel, forest debris, tree trunks, and huge boulders. Sometimes it destroyed regular bathing pools, creating new ones in the process. Finally, I arrived at the spot, believed to be where Mama Glo saw the demise of her victim. A huge tree had fallen across the river, over the basin. It was very mossy, so I refrained from walking over it, as I was alone. Studying the pool, I threw a rock in the middle to sound out its depth. I thought I heard a voice, keeping low and quiet I waited to see who would approach. After a short while no one showed, it must have been the forest whispering.

I sat on the riverbank and ate some oranges I had pilfered from an orange grove on my way. I ate oranges while listening to the forest communicate; the sounds of rustling leaves, singing birds and trees crying as their branches rubbed against each other. Boredom had begun to take a toll on me. I stripped off my clothes and gingerly ventured into the water. The water was freezing and much deeper near the bankside than I had expected. There was a steep slope, so I was forced to swim before my body could acclimatise to the temperature of the water. The cold water numbed my skin, but I soon adjusted to the temperature.

The water here wasn't as clear as where people normally gather to swim in the popular areas. There were lots of vines hanging from the trees on the banks. I tried to dive down to the bottom of the basin but panicked when I couldn't reach the riverbed because of submerged vines and branches. Resurfacing, I was gasping for breath in a panic. On my second attempt, I discovered that the riverbed was littered with dead leaves, trapped logs, branches, and vines. This would have made it very difficult to swim here leisurely. It was impossible for swimming near the bank because of the steep slopes. I did not want to be a pessimist, but I concluded from an unprofessional opinion that anyone swimming here alone was asking for trouble. Even if you swam here with friends, you could easily find yourself in difficulty. Especially if you were to get trapped in the network of underwater branches and vines lodged out of sight. My calculated guess was the man who drowned there could have slipped off the bank and fallen into the river. A freak accident, maybe he panicked. Not realising the depth, he found himself in difficulty and subsequently drowned. With no Mama Glo in sight that day, it was the only conclusion I could surmise.

One of my first steady jobs was at a bar in the heart of Arima. I remembered the interview well. The tall light-skinned Indian man ushered me outside the bar when I went for the interview. He was eating an orange while throwing questions at me. About two minutes into the interview, he asked how old I was. Sixteen I replied nervously. I knew there was an age restriction on for working in bars and establishments retailing alcohol for consumption on the premises. He then fired away another question, "76 and how much make a 100?".

Without having to think, I said 24.

He looked me over and smiled, "Okay, be here at eight o'clock sharp Monday morning. And, if anybody asks how old you are, just say seventeen". I was now given official authority to lie.

Working at the bar gave me a good, life education. The job also positioned me at a hub where access to folklore stories was aplenty. The bar was situated opposite the Arima market and next to an agricultural depot that purchased cocoa and coffee beans from farmers in the eastern district. So, there was always an abundance of supernatural stories bouncing around from the depths of the countryside. Most of these stories were narrated by people who always seem to be in a drunken state. This made it very difficult to match their stories with any sober tales, and these were far and few in between. At the end of the day, it *was* a bar. Nevertheless, every story had a peculiar twist and was worth a listening. Throughout the numerous sagas I had heard in the bar, not one person ever mentioned an encounter with Mama Glo. People did talk about Mama Glo, but no one related any first-hand experiences with this freshwater mermaid believed to be Papa Bois's companion. I gathered that not a lot of people may have met Mama Glo, or if they did it was to their demise so no real accounts of her were ever possible. Mama Glo would have to go down in the history books as one of the most elusive of Jumbies ever. People had seen Douens, Largahoo, La Diablesse and Soucouyant but very few had set eyes upon this aquatic Jumbie.

I first heard my mother speak of Mama Glo but her stories of Mama Glo always portrayed her as having snakes on her head instead of hair. This kind of contradiction with other stories and made had me confused to say the least. I heard and read tales in books and magazines about Mama Glo, but all were so vague to me. If Mama Glo did exist, she certainly was more elusive than Douen, Largahoo, La Diablesse, Papa Bois and Soucouyant put together. The other peculiar thing: Mama Glo, if legend was correct, had to reside near water to survive. Her survival would certainly be put into jeopardy should she stray far away from a river or lake for any rendezvous with Papa Bois. There was no way she could venture off anywhere without legs. As far as legend has it, she didn't fly. She could hardly even contemplate visiting her saltwater cousins on the coastlines.

For a short time, I worked for one of the country's leading construction companies building and resurfacing roads across Trinidad. We were constructing some roads in Longdenville, at a new agricultural project, experimenting with animal feed from sugarcane. There were lots of rice paddies and sugarcane fields close by and a fair bit of forested area too. The foreman, along with some of the other workers, would disappear every lunch time, returning with several bottles of *babash*, an illegally distilled rum. One day on their return, the foreman said to us that they saw a Mama Glo sitting on a log near a pond. Curious, I asked if they approached her. My foreman informed me the pond was infested with alligators, so naturally they wouldn't go near the water. On hearing this, I asked my foreman to accompany them the next time they went to purchase *babash*. As ill luck would have it, police raided the illegal distillery, seizing all the equipment and supposedly destroying whatever stock of *babash* that was ready for distribution. This police raid halted these regular lunch time rendezvous to purchase this locally distilled brew.

Not to be put off from my expedition to find Mama Glo, I persuaded the foreman – with a bottle of rum – to take me where they had spotted Mama Glo. He agreed almost instantly, indicating that tomorrow we would make the trip. The following day he brought a shotgun to work, with about six 12-gauge rounds. When I questioned him about the gun, he said it was for the alligators. He said alligators made good meat, especially the tail. I had heard of people eating alligator before but knew of no one who had consumed the meat before. In fact, I was very much still sceptical about alligator meat.

We drove for about two miles in a yellow van along this narrow country road, having to pull over precariously on the soft verge to allow oxen carts to pass. There was this tall Indian guy who alluded to have seen Mama Glo as well. He told me it was him who spotted Mama Glo and not the foreman. He also boasted to be a crack shot. I had to take his word on that as no one, including me, had ever seen him shoot. Maybe the foreman had confidence in his shooting because he relinquished the gun to him. He loaded the gun and broke it for safety.

The driver parked the yellow van in a little clearing, leaving ample room for other vehicles to manoeuvre. We walked for about twenty minutes through some dense woods, along a narrow track. To the left of us there was a clearing, and I could see the pond dotted with blooming lotus flowers. On the edges of the pond was tall reeds and verdant grass, in the middle of the pond, a fallen tree. The hairs on the back of my neck stood to attention, we were all very quiet. Why? I had no clue. The foreman tapped me on the shoulder, in a whisper he said. 'Look over there by the branch you will see the head.' In all honesty, I was expecting to see the head of Mama Glo. Instead, all I saw was the head of an alligator. I had seen alligators before, but this was the biggest Caiman I had ever laid eyes on. The Indian angled the shotgun, groomed his thick moustache, and took aim at the beast. I was thinking to myself, if they shoot, surely Mama Glo would not come out.

This tall, lanky Indian must have read my mind, we all stooped behind the tall grass and waited. Suddenly, there was a kind of croaking sound coming from different directions in the pond. The foreman held up three fingers, suggesting that there might be three alligators. Quietly, we all stood up, as if choreographed. The alligator was still there on the log with half of its body submerged and its head just above the water.

The Indian guy took aim and fired. He was indeed a crack shot. The alligator was splashing about the pond, its head shattered from the blast. One brave young man waded into the water to retrieve the beast now laying still, its head gone. That afternoon, the foreman roasted the tail over an open fire. I tasted alligator for the first time in my life, and it was delicious. A flaky consistency like cod fish. The crew had found a new supplier for *babash* and it brought a delightful end to the day before heading home after an honest day's work.

As I reflected on Mama Glo, being the protector of the aquatic life, she certainly was absent when one of her flock had met its untimely death from a shotgun cartridge. I was given a piece of the alligator meat to take home, which I accepted with some reluctance. When I got home, my partner at the time took one look at it wrapped in the newspaper and flung it out into the yard. The dog quickly grabbed it up, running off with other hounds hot on his heels. Some weeks later, the Indian guy said to me he didn't think it was Mama Glo they saw. He reckoned it could have been an alligator that was basking on the log. For some odd reason, my mind was leading me to believe this was so.

Interest in Mama Glo began to wane and the desire to embark on anymore wild goose chases faded. My instincts told me, too, that Mama Glo wouldn't be found at a pond. I had somehow envisaged that she would reside near running water. All other stories before had placed Mama Glo near rivers with swimming basins. On a personal level, I had grown weary of hunting these Jumbies without success. No amount of effort I put into tracking these folklore characters had brought an inkling of evidence to support the stories. These legendary and elusive creatures certainly knew how to avoid me.

One day out of the blue, a friend of mine, knowing of my interest in folklore said, "It have Mama Glo in Blanchisseuse". Someone had spotted Mama Glo near Marianne River. My enthusiasm perked up; Marianne River led to the sea. Maybe Mama Glo had gone up there to visit her saltwater cousins. I was excited about this prospect; I had never been to the river before. There was a suspension bridge over the river dating back from the colonial days, believed to be over a hundred years old. Although I had gone to Blanchisseuse many times, it was somewhere that I failed to visit on my excursions. I decided that this time I would make a leisure day of it and hike to Blanchisseuse.

To make the Blanchisseuse trip a leisurely one, I asked a couple of people if they were interested in doing the hike, about six people agreed. I was in the penultimate year of my teens, and I concocted this idea to have couples on the walk. That was the first thing that went wrong. On the day of the hike, we arranged to meet at the Dial in Arima. Instructions were to rendezvous at 6 am, with a 30-minute window for latecomers. At 6:05 I was already starting to become anxious and ready to leave. The next time I monitored the time it was 6:40 and only my trusted partner in crime had turned up. We both decided we would not wait a minute longer as the sun was already bearing down. We headed towards Mt Pleasant Road, buying some coconut cakes at the nearby bakery for the journey.

We passed the ice factory – where the woman was beheaded by my barber – at a steady pace. It wasn't long before we were nearing the Asa Wright Nature Reserve. The Reserve is home to more than 250 varieties of birds including the rare nocturnal fruit eating oilbird (*Steatornis caripensis),* known locally as guacharo. Roaming here freely you could also find the Red-rumped Agouti (*Dasyprocta leporina*), Ocelot (*Leopardus pardalis*) and Red Brocket Deer (*Mazama americana*). We were tempted to make a detour for a quick visit, but it's not the sort of place where you can spend ten minutes. It is about 300 hundred acres of natural beauty, attracting ornithologists, nature lovers, and tourists from all over the world, as well as local visitors.

At this point, I was relieved that the others didn't turn up, and my friend vocalised the same thought; "If we were six walking we would not have gotten this far, even if we started at 6".

I agreed, at this rate we could be in Blanchisseuse by midday I thought to myself. We got to a little junction, and I said to him maybe this is a shortcut. He laughed at me saying, "You go that way, and you end up in Lalaja". A small village that veered off into territory unknown to me. It was amazing that in such a small country, there were still places yet to explore.

We continued at a steady pace, encountering cocoa plantations on both sides of the road. I jumped over the slippery ditch and picked two brilliant yellow cocoa pods. We sucked on the pulpy seeds to give us energy as we picked up the pace. A few miles later we had brought our bad habits with us. My friend spotted a low coconut tree with a good crop of Chinese coconuts. He scrambled up the steep incline and wrenched two off the tree, throwing them down to me. We sat under a tree at the roadside, enjoying the cool water from the stolen coconuts and the cakes we had purchased earlier that morning.

I reckoned we may have passed the halfway mark to Blanchisseuse when we got a glimpse of the ocean through some clearing in the forest. It was only then that my friend spoke about Mama Glo.

"So, dis Mama Glo woman, yuh t'ink you will find she?".

All my endeavours to find a Jumbie, despite an open mind and a positive attitude, all ended in failure. Yet every time I embarked on a new hunt it was always with enthusiastic optimism. The answer burning the tip of my tongue to say to my friend was, no! Instead, I said to him, "People in Blanchisseuse say they have seen Mama Glo. I believe them, I don't think they would lie".

He began to laugh, "Boy these people does lie no ass. They always catching the biggest fish, seen the largest carite bird tiefing fish from pelican, and you believe them when they tell you they see Mama Glo?".

I had to remind him that it was he who alerted me to the notion that Mama Glo was spotted in Marianne River. He did however have a valid point, but I kept my optimism intact. He turned to me and said with the most deadpan stare, "To ass with this hiking stupidness. The next vehicle come by, we flagging it down".

I couldn't have agreed with him more on the decision. Although I was enjoying the walk, lethargy was beginning to take hold of my legs. I wanted to get there in good time also so we could enjoy a good swim in the sea as well.

An old moss green Bedford lorry braked, spurting thick black smoke from the exhaust, fouling the air with the fumes of diesel. We jumped on the back of the truck, loaded with foodstuff and several cartoons of beer and Guinness. Everything was secured with blue nylon rope. Once we got into Blanchisseuse, I called on a friend who I work with a few years ago. We arrived just as they were serving up fish stew and dumplings. The aroma of the food was heavenly, and it was a delicious repast. Once we had eaten and quenched our thirst with ice cold sorrel drink, I mentioned my purpose to Blanchisseuse to my friend. He was enthusiastic about the prospect of finding Mama Glo too. He warned that it was impossible to spot Mama Glo near the pools, too many people gather there to swim so Mama Glo won't venture anywhere near.

"I know a place where people have seen Mama Glo", he said pulling on a pair of rubber boots, "We go by boat".

The prospect of the boat excited us both and looked forward to the adventure. It was a short walk to Marianne River from my friend's house. We went over the suspension bridge which no longer supported motor traffic. Leaving the bridge, we made our way through some bushes along the riverbank where a small fibreglass boat was tied to a tree. The boat was painted in an aquamarine blue. Painted in black bold letters, on both sides were the words, *River Jamette*. There was a deflated look of disappointment when we saw the flimsy little boat, barely large enough to take three people. Nevertheless, the boat launched, and we started to row this jamette upriver. Our chatter became whispers, heads tucked low to avoid the low hanging branches and bamboo over the river. After about twenty minutes, we came across a flat bank to one side of the river where there were lots of flowers and other bits that looked like offerings.

"What's all that?", I questioned.

Without breaking the rhythm of his strokes my friend explained that the Hindus come here every year to celebrate the Ganga Dhara Teerath (river festival). They offer prayers to Ganga Mai (mother of the river). It is thought that up to 20,000 buttercups and marigolds are offered in the yearly ritual, that dates back thousands of years in the Hindu calendar. This fascinated me as I had never heard of it before. The festival must have been recent because the yellow hues of the flowers were still vibrant along the river's edge.

Rowing into a little inlet, trees and bamboo clusters created a canopy over the water. We stopped rowing and, in a whisper, the boat man said, "My uncle said he saw Mama Glo here once, sitting on that log combing her hair".

Slowly, and in stealthy stillness he pushed the boat along the shallow water with the oar. The surroundings were eerie, I felt goose bumps for the first time. The lush green forest all around us was alive with the sound of birds and I could distinctively hear the howl of a monkey in the distance. We waited and waited, but Mama Glo never showed. Turning the boat around we proceeded to another curve in the river. Here the water was divided by a ridge of gravel in the middle and the forest, seemingly bowing to have a drink in the clean clear water. My hiking companion said, "This place gives me the creeps man!"

It wasn't scary but the quiet flow of the water and the serene surrounding was not only beautiful, but it was also haunting, in a romantic kind of way. I couldn't help but remember the remnants of the Ganga Dhara that we saw earlier. Suddenly, we heard a splash in the water and a little cry. On a log half submerged in a deep pool, we saw something sitting on the log, preening. The boat moved silently and nearer. As we got close enough to get a better glimpse, we saw it was an otter chomping away at a freshly caught fish. The otter spotted us and soon made off further up the river. "We call them water dog. Is ah big one though," the boat man said.

We had been on the river for about two hours prowling suspected inlets and bank side searching for Mama Glo. We sailed back in the direction we came and went under the suspension bridge, following the river as it made its way to the sea. There were swimmers wading about and young boys in oversized shorts were jumping into the water from the high bank on one side. Further down the river we pulled up to a flat area and disembarked. We helped to haul the *River Jamette* from the water and carry her to a nearby house where it was left with its hull facing up. It was a short walk to Marianne Bay where we swam until the sun had completed its task for the day. My friend, riding one of the swells, shouted above the roar of the waves, "Mama Glo outsmart you again boy".

Dipping under a wave, I ignored him completely.

Having enjoyed a good swim, we walked to the main road. By now, our trunks were dry, and we went to the nearby local bar and drank beers until the bus to Arima arrived. As we were making our way to the bus to head back to Arima, my friend shouted, "Why allyuh don't stay the night.

Leatherback turtles coming up on the beach tonight to lay their eggs."

My friend's uncle had started organising patrols to stop hunters killing the turtles for their meat and harvesting the eggs. We all headed back to the bar and waited for the vigil to begin. Putting his hand on my shoulders, my Blanchisseuse friend said, "You never know, you miss Mama Glo, but a good night for seeing Soucouyant."

Jumbie Come to Meet You

Working at the bar one day, this skinny *cocopanyol* called Jesus, said to me, "I hear you looking for Papa Bois?".

I served him his *petit quart* of rum and he poured it all into the glass. Dipping his index finger into the glass, he licked it, and continued, "I am Papa Bois you know".

Now this man was much older than me by scores. He always wore a machete sheathed in a brown leather case and khaki clothing. I got the feeling too, that he even slept with the machete strapped to his person. I looked at him with some scepticism as he savoured the rum with this finger dipping method. I was petrified when he drew his machete from the case, banging it on the laminated counter, shouting, "I am Papa Bois!"

Someone in the bar shouted back, "Jesus haul yuh ass and go back in de bush."

Jesus looked at me. He banged his chest with his two fists like King Kong. Gazing at me with glaring eyes, he whispered, "I am Papa Bois yuh know." There was this innocent pleading in his eyes for me to believe he was Papa Bois. I smiled as he poured the rum down his throat, turn the glass upside down on the counter and left quietly. I never saw Jesus after that incident.

For all my diligence and the vicious floggings from my mother as a young boy searching for these folklore legends, none of my endeavours produced a result. From the initial chopping of the Silk Cotton tree to the relentless search for Douens, Largahoo, Soucouyant, La Diablesse and Mama Glo, nothing came as close as the sighting of the hovering light. To this day, I have never seen anything like it ever again. The Cumuto woman, suspected of being a Soucouyant had not gone back to Grenada as my girlfriend's brother had alluded. She was alive and well, living in Arima, doing a brisk spice trade in the market. Someone told me she also had a stall near Charlotte Street in Port of Spain. There were other people who sold spices, so I never really knew who she was, or what she looked like.

My friend's mother, who I first suspected of being a Soucouyant had since died, and I kid you not when I tell you that whenever I went to the late show at cinema and walked home, I was positive that a figure in her guise with a white head tie could be seen standing at the front of her yard. This wasn't my eyes playing tricks on me for others had reported similar sightings of that description. That road itself was regarded as a haunted one. An elderly man riding home late one night from a wake, told how he came face to face with a Largahoo under the huge Balata (*Manilkara bidentate*) tree that hung over the road. People claimed to have seen Soucouyant flying about at night too.

What I do remember as the most chilling experience was that night when I stayed up with my mother while she did the washing. There was a genuine fright in my mother's eyes, and while I did not see anything, the presence of something unnatural loomed in the darkness. After that night, my mother sounded a caution that we should enter the house facing backwards to ensure no evil spirits followed us into the house.

My mother was full of superstitions. In the early days when I began Jumbie hunting she had taken me to an Obeah woman who lived on the other side of Arima. This woman gave me a bath with a concoction of some local bushes including *shinning bush, black sage, sweetgrass, wild carali, vervine* and a cube of blue - something people used to rinse white clothes with when washing. The Obeah woman repeatedly whipped me with a broom made of Cocoyea and sweetgrass, chanting a prayer as she performed the exorcism. She broke an egg on my head and continued whipping me, pouring the bush mixture over my naked body as I stood in a metal bath pan. My mother parted with $15 and a flask of white rum. This seemed to please both the Obeah woman and my mother. Two days later I was out again looking for Douens.

In retrospect, the Obeah woman must have done a good job on me to ward off evil spirits. Maybe this was the reason I failed to encounter any of the evil dwellers of Trinidadian folklore. Some months later, I got my own back on the Obeah woman. I stole one of her chickens along with a small bottle of white rum she had placed near one of the shrines in the yard. Two other truants joined me, we cooked the chicken and drank the white rum with much relish.

A general Census in the early 1980s in Trinidad meant that places that did not have running water or electricity became illuminated with electric light. Newly created roadways replaced tracks and muddy traces with tarmac roads as well as concrete drains. This new development created housing settlements and so, common sightings of folklore creatures such as Largahoo, Douen, La Diablesse and Soucouyant became less frequent. You hardly ever heard of anyone being attacked by a Soucouyant while they slept at night anymore.

The folklore, however, never ceased to be part of the culture and traditions of Trinidad and Tobago. The widespread use of television across the country meant that programmes were made about these folklores that kept the stories alive.   Only recently, I saw a documentary on YouTube portraying young man setting crab traps near a mangrove. He claimed to have seen Papa Bois watching him from behind some mangrove vegetation. It just goes to show that the cultural traditions of these folklores are very much an innate fabric of the culture in Trinidad and Tobago. Not only are these traditions passed on through the griot method or electronic media in modern day, but they have also been kept alive in our carnival traditions too. Carnival costumes depicting characters such as Papa Bois, Mama Glo, Soucouyant, La Diablesse and Largahoo often form part of carnival costume traditions that play an integral part of incorporating history and culture.

While my search for these folklore creatures of supernatural existence never came to any fruition, the experiences and adventures far outweigh the disappointment I initially felt.   Today, I feel proud to know that these folklores have not died with the new generation of people coming through. Despite the advent of the digital age and the electronification of societies through various platforms of social media, folklore is very much still alive. The traditions of folklore tales still play a very vibrant part in the Caribbean, as it does in Trinidad and Tobago.

One of my regrets, however, has been the lack of knowledge about East Indian folklore. It would have been a great learning experience to know more about what the Indian indentured labourers brought with them in terms of their supernatural experiences. What I did learn through my experiences was how folklore has played a part in shaping our interaction with the environment that we live in. Had we heeded some of these stories and traditions, taking to time to understand our purpose and existence, maybe we could have been teaching the world a thing or two about environmental sustainability. The protection of our forests was a job left up to Papa Bois to sustain the longevity for future generations, preserving the habitat that we are constantly destroying as our greed intensifies, pillaging the earth of the resources that sustains us.

I presume the erosion of our forest, in the quest for financial benefits and the populating of urban and rural countryside, has made it even more difficult to spot a Largahoo, Douen, Soucouyant, Papa Bois, La Diablesse or Mama Glo. Wherever they are, these folklore characters must be sitting, laughing, reminiscing on that folly of a young boy trying to find them. Maybe they are thinking too, should we have presented ourselves to him? In that way people would have taken heed and cared more for the environment that surrounds them, we will never know.

Still, as I write, almost five decades after my inquisitive premonitions took hold, I have not known or met a single person who could whole-heartedly say that they had come face-to-face with a Largahoo, Douen, La Diablesse, Soucouyant, Papa Bois or his companion, Mama Glo. Nor did I ever meet anyone who had successfully chopped a Silk Cotton tree to witness blood oozing from its robust thorn-studded trunk.

My mother used to love saying the following with a hint of sarcasm: "What eh miss yuh eh pass yuh". Back then understanding her little parables was beyond my grasp. Maybe, understanding her words now, I could still hold out for the odd chance of spotting one of these folklore legends. Who knows, when I roam the city of Port of Spain or any other country towns or lanes in the ungodly hours of the night, there just might be an opportunity to see a Jumbie in town.

Other Book by The Author

About the Author

David Kalloo was born in Port of Spain, Trinidad. He spent most of his impressionable years growing up between Arima and San Juan where he attended a Seventh Day Adventist School.

Having left formal education at the age of 14 he drifted through variuos methods of employment before becoming a self-taught signwriter. Growing up in a diverse society like Trinidad, where the exposure and, more importantly, the participation in all its cultures helped to elevate his understanding and appreciation of its society in general.

This complexity of inter-mingling ethnicity and cultural honeycomb played a crucial part in his life when he migrated to London in 1989, in the hopes of expanding his knowledge in the sign industry. Unfortunately the career path of a signwriter was not to be and adapting to meet family needs saw this profession drifted from his path.

David spent many years with a costume band at the Notting Hill Carnival and in 2001 focussed his interest in documenting the history of Notting Hill Carnival. This venture played a dynamic role when he embarked on an undergraduate study in Caribbean Studies and Media Studies at London Metropolitan university. Wading into full time Higher Education, after 31 years had its challenges however, it also awaken a dormant passion for writing. He has published a concised version of the history of Notting Hill Carnival in the Trinidad and Tobago High Commission's *Newsletter* and several articles on carnival an soca music in the London magazine *SocaNews*.

Having completed his BA in Caribbean Studies and Media Studies in 2008, he recently graduated with an MA in International Relation. David has been a judge with the Notting Hill carnival for 3 consecutive years and also judged Hackney One Carnival. He also sat on a judging panel for a short story competition in conjuction with Black History Month 2017, organised by a leading city Law firm. He is the founder and editor of the online magazine, *Culturepulse*. A publication dedicated to connecting the people of the Caribbean Diaspora.

David has served as a Trustee with Steelpan Trust, The Trinidad and Tobago Association UK and currently the Communications and Media advisor with the FHALMA Foundation, the Media Manager for the Notting Hill Carnival Pioneers festival. David has written three books *Green Mango Chow*, *Does the Crime Epidemic in Trinidad and Tobago Cast a Negative Impact on the Country's Economy, Regionally and Internationally?* and a contributing chapter in; *Celebrating Trinidad and Tobago's Culture and the Arts,*

Printed in Great Britain
by Amazon

33796779R00079